Mesopotamian Mythology

A Captivating Guide to Ancient Near Eastern Myths

© Copyright 2019

All Rights Reserved. No part of this book may be reproduced in any form without permission in writing from the author. Reviewers may quote brief passages in reviews.

Disclaimer: No part of this publication may be reproduced or transmitted in any form or by any means, mechanical or electronic, including photocopying or recording, or by any information storage and retrieval system, or transmitted by email without permission in writing from the publisher.

While all attempts have been made to verify the information provided in this publication, neither the author nor the publisher assumes any responsibility for errors, omissions or contrary interpretations of the subject matter herein.

This book is for entertainment purposes only. The views expressed are those of the author alone, and should not be taken as expert instruction or commands. The reader is responsible for his or her own actions.

Adherence to all applicable laws and regulations, including international, federal, state and local laws governing professional licensing, business practices, advertising and all other aspects of doing business in the US, Canada, UK or any other jurisdiction is the sole responsibility of the purchaser or reader.

Neither the author nor the publisher assumes any responsibility or liability whatsoever on behalf of the purchaser or reader of these materials. Any perceived slight of any individual or organization is purely unintentional.

Free Bonus from Captivating History (Available for a Limited time)

Hi History Lovers!

Now you have a chance to join our exclusive history list so you can get your first history ebook for free as well as discounts and a potential to get more history books for free! Simply visit the link below to join.

Captivatinghistory.com/ebook

Also, make sure to follow us on Facebook, Twitter and Youtube by searching for Captivating History.

Contents

INTRODUCTION 1
PART I: CREATION MYTHS 5
PART II: TALES OF GODS AND GODDESSES 30
PART III: SELECTIONS FROM THE *EPIC OF GILGAMESH* 51
GLOSSARY 79
BIBLIOGRAPHY 88

Introduction

The civilizations that grew up in the Tigris and Euphrates River Valleys many thousands of years ago have left important legacies: agriculture, mathematics, astronomy, the wheel, and writing. The ancient Sumerian culture was one of the first to create a method of recording thoughts and data in a more or less permanent form, and other peoples who came into contact with the Sumerians adopted this idea for their own uses. Not only did they adopt technological advances, but also there was a great deal of interplay between Sumerian mythology and storytelling and that of Mesopotamian culture, generally.

Starting around 2300 BCE, Akkadian became the standard language of the Mesopotamian region, and it was split into three dialects: spoken Akkadian fell into either the northern or Assyrian dialect, or the southern or Babylonian dialect, while a third literary dialect was in use for written works and thus was accessible only to the educated. A Semitic language that is related to modern Arabic, Amharic, and Hebrew, Akkadian was used to record business transactions, laws, history and pseudo-history, mythology, and heroic epics. It was the language of trade and diplomacy for a wide geographical area as well, extending both into a large part of western Asia and even into northwest Africa. For example, we have surviving pedagogical documents showing that scribes in ancient

Egypt might be expected to learn to read and write Akkadian as part of their duties.

Mesopotamia also was the scene for a series of imperial projects, starting with the Akkadian Empire under Sargon of Akkad in the 24th century BCE. Akkad was a city-state, the exact location of which has yet to be determined, and from this base Sargon expanded his reach to other places including Sumer. After the fall of the Akkadian Empire, the city-states of Assur (the primary city of Assyria) in the north and Babylon in the south vied for control of the region, each having success at various times.

Because of the linguistic, political, and religious intermingling of speakers of the Akkadian language, it is very difficult to separate out specific religious or mythological traditions for any of these three cultures, with certain exceptions. We know that the principal deity of Assyria was the god Assur, and the principal deity of Babylon was Marduk. There are certain creation legends that can be connected specifically with Babylon because of the primacy of Marduk in those tales, and certain prayers and incantations addressed to Assur that obviously come from Assyria, but it is otherwise extremely difficult to parse which mythographic bits came from which culture due to the roster of shared divinities in the pantheon, the sharing of myths, and the commonalities of religious practices among Mesopotamian peoples. The waters are further muddied by the integration of Sumerian, Assyrian, and Babylonian mythographic practices; many of the clay tablets containing these stories are bilingual, in both Sumerian and Akkadian, while myths in these languages also contain many parallels in terms of character, theme, and plot.

Surviving documents in Akkadian principally are in cuneiform writing on clay tablets. The word "cuneiform" comes from the Latin *cuneus*, which means "wedge," referring to the use of a wedge-shaped stylus to impress symbols into wet clay. The Sumerians originated this form of writing, which was later adapted for the Akkadian language. A significant number of literary texts come from royal libraries that were compiled by the Assyrian king Sennacherib

(705–681 BCE) and Ashurbanipal (r. 668–c. 627 BCE), the king of the so-called Neo-Assyrian Empire. The ruins of these libraries, in what is now Iraq, were discovered by archaeologists in the mid-nineteenth century, and until that time, writings from these ancient civilizations had been lost to history. Therefore, the modern discipline of Assyriology (a blanket term for studies of the ancient Near East) is less than two hundred years old, and more is yet to be discovered from the fragments that have been excavated (or pillaged) from the remains of these ancient civilizations. One recent discovery from 2015 is a new segment of the *Epic of Gilgamesh*.

This present volume of Mesopotamian myths is divided into three sections. The first of these contains creation myths, the most extended of which is the *Enuma Elish*, or Babylonian creation story. In this myth, the god Marduk does battle with the dragon Tiamat, and from her body and that of her second-in-command, he creates the world. The story of Atrahasis involves not original creation but re-creation, since this is the myth of the Great Flood that the gods send to wash everything away. The good man Atrahasis is spared only by the intervention of the god Enki, who forewarns Atrahasis and tells him to build the ark that will save him, his family, and the animals. Etana's tale is less cosmic in nature than the preceding two stories: the act of creation involved is Etana's attempt to have a child and thus an heir to his throne.

The deeds and foibles of the Mesopotamian gods are on display in the second section, in stories that inform us about the characters of these divinities and which contain themes that tell us something about Mesopotamian concepts of cosmic order. In the first story, the goddess Ishtar decides to visit the Underworld where the goddess Ereshkigal holds sway. When Ereshkigal worries that Ishtar plans to supplant her, she sets a trap that holds Ishtar prisoner until she is rescued. Ereshkigal's deed has cosmic implications: since Ishtar is a fertility goddess, her imprisonment means that procreation on Earth is suspended.

Ereshkigal is a primary figure in the next story as well, which tells how Nergal, god of war and pestilence, comes to be her consort. Nergal manages to refuse all of the blandishments Ereshkigal puts before him, except for the enticement of her body. Having given into his desire, Nergal must make the Underworld his abode and remain there as Ereshkigal's lover or else Ereshkigal will overturn the natural order by sending the dead onto the Earth to eat the living.

Divine and natural order are also themes of the last two stories in this section. In the first, the hero-god Ninurta does his own work of restoring divine order when he defeats the Anzu Bird who steals the Tablets of Destiny from Ellil, while the myth about Adapa functions as a just-so story explaining why humans are not immortal.

Perhaps the most famous of all Mesopotamian myths is the *Epic of Gilgamesh*, an extended narrative about the exploits of Gilgamesh, king of Uruk, and his wild-man friend, Enkidu. If the stories of the gods told in the first two sections function as explanations about cosmic order, the themes of *Gilgamesh* center on the internal order of human beings, focusing on the deep love and friendship between Enkidu and Gilgamesh, on human fears about mortality, and the human desire for eternal life.

Mesopotamian myths are some of the oldest written stories in the world, and although in modern history we have only had the privilege of knowing them for less than two hundred years, they nevertheless speak to us about things that are basic to the human condition. Love, hate, creation, destruction, desire, sorrow, and fear are all universal human experiences and have been since the beginning of time, as is the human wish to project these things onto beings that are larger than life in order to explain how the world came to be the way it is.

Part I: Creation Myths

The Creation of the World

The Babylonian creation myth is preserved in cuneiform writing on seven clay tablets and has come to be known as the Enuma Elish, *after the first two words of the epic. In ancient times, this important myth was recited annually on the Babylonian New Year in honor of Marduk, the primary Babylonian god, who defeats the rebellious goddess Tiamat and her general, the god Qingu. Marduk then uses the bodies of his slain enemies to create the heavens and the Earth, and to make human beings to serve the gods.*

Unfortunately, the tablets that preserve the Enuma Elish *are broken and incomplete, so much of the original poem is missing. However, the poem tends to repeat large sections of text, so what is missing from one point in the story sometimes can be recreated or inferred from another. The myth recounts the emergence or creation of several named gods, the most important of whom are Marduk and his father, Ea. In addition to Marduk and his immediate ancestors, many other gods both named and unnamed have roles in this tale, but their origin stories are not told here.*

In the time when the heavens above had no name and the Earth beneath had no name, there was only Apsu, the one who begat the heavens and the Earth, and with Apsu was Tiamat, who gave birth to them. And in this time, the waters mingled together, the sweet water that was Apsu and the salt that was Tiamat, but neither was there pasture nor reeded marsh, nor had any of the gods yet been begotten or given names.

Then it happened that the gods came into being. First among them were Lahmu and Lahamu, brother and sister, the children of Apsu and Tiamat, and Lahmu and Lahamu together are the constellations in the sky. From Lahmu and Lahamu came Anshar and Kishar, brother and sister, god of the sky and goddess of the Earth. If Lahmu and Lahamu were great, Anshar and Kishar were greater yet, greater of stature, greater of strength.

From Anshar and Kishar came Anu, the very equal of his divine father, and Anu begat Ea, the god of the waters of the Tigris and the Euphrates. Ea was even greater than his own father, was even mightier than his own grandfather, and the wisdom of Ea knew no bounds.

Together Ea and his brother gods roared up and down the divine abode. Such a clamor they made that it disturbed Tiamat. In the face of their doings, Tiamat held her peace, although she detested their acts. Such a noise the brother gods made that even Apsu could not make himself heard above it, and so Apsu called to himself Mummu, his adviser, and said, "Good Mummu, let us go to Tiamat and take counsel together. We must decide what to do with these gods who roar up and down our divine abode."

And so Mummu and Apsu went to Tiamat, and Apsu said, "We must have order! We must have peace! Surely I should destroy these brother gods who roar up and down our divine abode."

But Tiamat replied, "Destruction is too harsh a solution. We should not destroy what we ourselves have created. Let us deal kindly with the brother gods, to make them stop their roaring about."

Mummu spoke next. "Yes, O Apsu, O radiant one, surely you must destroy these gods. Destroy them all! Then you will have peace, then you will have order in the divine abode."

Then Apsu rejoiced, for he knew that Mummu spoke the truth. Apsu rejoiced and plotted to kill all his children, and Mummu fell upon Apsu's neck and embraced him.

But the plans of Apsu did not go unnoticed. Ea learned of what Apsu meant to do and vowed to put a stop to the destruction of the brother gods. Ea crafted a great spell, a powerful spell, a holy spell of sleep, and he cast it upon Apsu. Apsu was powerless to resist the incantation, and soon he fell into a deep slumber. When Ea saw that Apsu was overcome with sleep, he went to Apsu and took from him his diadem and put it upon his own brow. Ea bound Apsu with strong bonds, and then Ea slew that elder god. Ea slew Apsu, the father of all the gods, and then he fell upon Mummu and bound him in chains and threw him into a strong room, locking the door so that there should be no escape.

Then it was that Ea founded a divine abode of his own. He founded this abode and called it the *Apsu*. Within this abode, Ea made a chamber, a chamber for himself and for his wife, Damkina. And there it was in the abode called the Apsu that Marduk was begotten. Ea was his father, and Damkina was his mother. Marduk, the greatest of gods, was begotten there, and his father Ea delighted in him. Ea bestowed great majesty and strength upon Marduk, making him not only the equal of the other gods but their superior. Well made in his body was Marduk, with comely limbs. Four eyes had Marduk, and four ears, and from his mouth shot flames of fire. Large were his eyes and ears, and his body was exceeding tall, and he was named Son of the Sun and Sun of the Heavens, and his father Ea delighted in him greatly.

Anu, god of the sky and father of Ea, fashioned the four winds. Anu took these winds and gave them to his grandson, Marduk. Anu gave the winds to Marduk, and with these Marduk called up a mighty storm. The storm made waves upon waves, and this disturbed Tiamat greatly.

The other gods saw what was done, and they went to Tiamat, saying, "Did not Ea destroy Apsu, your divine spouse? Did he not imprison Mummu, Apsu's wise counsellor? And so it is that now we cannot sleep. And so it is that we have no rest. Come! Let us go into battle! Let us avenge Apsu and Mummu and recover our peace that we may rest."

And so the gods went aside to plan their battle.

But Tiamat, for her part, engendered great monsters, strong beasts and fell, that they might avenge her divine spouse, that they might destroy Ea and thus punish him for his deeds. Tiamat brought forth dragons, beasts with poisonous sharp teeth, creatures so fearsome that even the bravest would die if they but saw them. Dragons Tiamat brought forth, and many other beasts besides: lions and scorpion-men, wild dogs and demons, and a great bull. Eleven of these beasts Tiamat brought forth, but she gave the headship to none of these, preferring instead to bestow it on her son, Qingu. To him, Tiamat gave the three Tablets of Destiny, that he might have the power to overthrow Ea.

Then Tiamat said to Qingu, "Go! Lead the army of fell beasts! Lead the army of gods who are our allies! Bring battle to Ea, and avenge my divine spouse!"

Word of what Tiamat had done came to Ea, and he despaired. Surely he would never defeat such an army, headed by such a captain. Ea went to his grandfather, Anshar, and said, "Woe! Tiamat has created an army of eleven fell beasts, and of many gods, with Qingu at their head, and he bears the Tablets of Destiny. Surely we will never prevail against such a foe!"

Anshar said, "No, we shall not falter! You yourself slew Apsu, Tiamat's divine spouse. Any foe that faces you surely will be defeated. Go into battle!"

And so Ea set out to do battle with Tiamat. He found the place where she was with her army, and when he saw how very great the fell monsters were, with Qingu at their head, he grew greatly afraid, and he turned back.

"O my father," said Ea, "I set out on my road to do battle with Tiamat, but woe! Her power is too much for me. I shall never be able to defeat her. Send someone else instead."

Then Anshar turned to Anu and said, "O my son, my firstborn! You who are hero and warrior, no one may withstand your strength. Go you and fight Tiamat and her army! Surely you shall return victorious!"

And so Anu set out to do battle with Tiamat, but when he saw what she had prepared against him, his heart quailed, and he turned back.

"O my father," said Anu, "I set out on my road to do battle with Tiamat, but woe! Her power is too much for me. I shall never be able to defeat her. Perhaps you yourself should go."

Anshar called to himself all the gods. He told them of Tiamat's plans and of the army she had created, how they purposed to destroy all the other gods in revenge for the death of Apsu. But none of the other gods would take up the quest to defeat her. They all sat silent and afraid.

It was then that Ea summoned his son, Marduk. Together they went into Ea's chamber to take counsel together. Ea said, "Only you may stand against Tiamat and her fell beasts. Go before Anshar. Declare yourself our champion. Only you can save us!"

Obedient to his father, Marduk went before Anshar and the other gods. There he declared himself their champion, there he offered to meet Tiamat and her fell beasts, with Qingu at their head. Then the gods rejoiced and declared a feast, a feast to celebrate Marduk, their champion, before he went into battle. And when the feast was done, they said, "Marduk our champion shall be first among us! To you shall be the sovereignty over all that is, and even the gods shall bow down to you."

And so it was that Marduk readied himself for war. He took up his great bow and a quiver of arrows. He took up his mighty spear and his massive club. He took up lightning and filled his whole body with flame. He commanded the winds to help him, the four winds and the seven winds. These and other winds besides he called to him, to come with him and to wreak havoc on Tiamat. To his chariot he harnessed four steeds, swift as arrows and fierce as lions. Thus prepared, Marduk set out for battle in his chariot pulled by war stallions, with the winds at his command.

Qingu heard the approach of Marduk and saw him thus arrayed for battle, and his heart quailed. Seeing their leader's distress, the eleven fell beasts also despaired, but Tiamat gathered her courage and spoke words of rebellion to Marduk.

Marduk was not swayed by the words of Tiamat. He said to her, "You have rebelled against Anu, against the gods themselves. You have prepared an army to destroy them. But I say to you that we should settle this between ourselves. Let us meet in single combat, you and I, and that way decide who may have the victory."

For answer, Tiamat screamed her battle cry and ran at Marduk, thinking to destroy him where he stood. Not fearing her at all, Marduk held his ground. He took up a great net and threw it over Tiamat, entangling her so that she could not move. Then Marduk sent an evil wind to blow in Tiamat's face, to force open her mouth and to distend her body so that she could not speak. When that was done, Marduk nocked an arrow to his bow and shot Tiamat. The arrow entered her and clove her heart in two.

When Tiamat's army saw what had befallen the goddess, the eleven beasts fled the field. The gods who had followed Tiamat trembled and tried to flee, but Marduk caught them all in his net and threw them into prison. The demons also that had followed in Tiamat's train Marduk captured, and he hunted down the eleven beasts and cast them into fetters. Last of all, Marduk captured Qingu. Marduk took from him the Tablets of Destiny and fastened them upon his own breast.

Then Marduk went to the body of the slain Tiamat. With his great club, Marduk crushed her skull. He cut open the vessels of her body and let the North Wind take her blood away. The other gods rejoiced at Marduk's victory, giving him many fine gifts and praising him well.

But Marduk's work was not yet done. He took Tiamat's body and cut it in half along its length. One half of her body he set above to be the sky. Marduk posted two guardians to watch that portion of Tiamat, to make sure that the waters it contained did not escape. This done, Marduk went into the heavens, and there he created an abode for the gods. This abode he built neighboring the Apsu that his father Ea had made, and Marduk called his dwelling the *E-sara*. The E-sara was made to be even greater than the Apsu, and within the E-sara, Marduk made dwelling places for his grandfather, Anu, and for his father, Ea, and for Ellil, the god of the winds.

That done, Marduk began a new work. In the sky, he placed the stars in their courses; he made the twelve creatures of the Zodiac and put them in their rightful places. Marduk divided the times and the seasons, he created the calendar of months and days, and to watch over this, he placed Nibiru [the planet Jupiter]. Marduk created Nanna, the moon-god, and commanded him to shine at his proper time. To Nanna, Marduk gave the keeping of time, the measure of the months, and the times and places he should stand in relation to Shamash, the sun-god, and thus it was that Marduk established the turnings of the night and the day and the turnings of the months and the years.

From Tiamat's body, Marduk made the waters. He made the rain and the mist; he filled the abyss with the waters from her head. Two rivers he made flow from her eyes, the great rivers of the Tigris and the Euphrates, and from her breasts, Marduk wrought the mountains.

And so it was that from Tiamat's body was made the substance of the Earth.

When all was ready, Marduk gave the guiding of the world to his father Ea, and to his grandfather, Anu, he gave the Tablets of Destiny that he had taken from Qingu. The eleven fell beasts made by Tiamat he bound, and he made statues of them to guard the gates of the Apsu.

Seeing all that Marduk had done, all the gods rejoiced. They proclaimed the glory of his name; they gave him rich gifts. The gods all bowed down to Marduk and honored him greatly. They clothed him in clean robes and anointed him with fragrant oil. They gave to him the keeping of their holy places, and they said to him, "You alone shall be our king! Whatever you command, thus shall we do!"

Then Marduk said, "The Apsu I have made secure, and the E-sara I have made to be your abode. But another palace shall I yet create, the place where the gods shall gather to take counsel together. This place shall I call *Babylon*. In Babylon shall we make feast, and in Babylon shall we receive the offerings that we are due."

And the council of the gods said, "Yes, all these things you should do, for you are our king, and we shall have none other. Let it be done as you say."

When things had been set in order in the heavens and on the Earth, Marduk bent his thought to the creation of other things, of things that might live and move upon the Earth. "I shall make a creature," said Marduk, "I shall make it of bone and of blood, and its duty shall be to provide for the gods. This creature I shall call 'man,' and I shall make it to live upon the Earth."

Then Marduk turned to the council of the gods and said, "Tell me, who was it that told Tiamat to rise in rebellion against us? Whose words swayed her and caused her to bring battle?"

The gods answered Marduk, saying, "Qingu it was who fomented rebellion, and Qingu it was who told Tiamat to bring battle."

Thus it was that Qingu was brought before Marduk and the council of the gods. Bound in fetters, Qingu was brought before them, and sentence was passed upon him. Marduk opened the vessels of his body, and from his blood, Marduk fashioned human beings to be the servants of the gods.

The heavens and the Earth had been created, and the sun and the moon given their duties. Human beings had been created to serve the gods, and all had been set in order except for the council of the gods themselves. Marduk divided the gods into companies and told them where they were to dwell. Three hundred he made to guard the heavens, and six hundred he sent to the Earth and to the Underworld.

When that was done, the gods turned to Marduk and said, "O King, you have done a great work. You have made all that is. You have created human beings to do service for us. What now might we do for you in return?"

Marduk was greatly pleased by what the gods had said, and he replied, "Create Babylon! Make for us a shrine in which we might repose ourselves."

The gods accepted this task with a good will. They went to work making bricks, and from the bricks, they made a city, and within the city, a great shrine was built, a high tower that was to be a temple where Marduk might reside along with Ea, Ellil, and Anu. For themselves also they built temples, that they might have places of repose.

Babylon soon was finished, a great and shining city with a fine temple to the gods. Marduk was well pleased with this work, and he said, "Well done, well done, my brother gods! Let us now have a feast! Let us eat and drink to celebrate our creations and to celebrate our new shrine in which we might repose."

The whole company of the gods sat down with Marduk to a feast. They ate and drank to their hearts' content. They rejoiced in the making of their new city and their new shrines. When the feasting was over, the gods took a solemn oath to Marduk, proclaiming him their king and judge, giving over to him dominion of all things. They also made commandments for the proper care for the gods and of the work that human beings ought to do in honor of all the deities. The gods all praised Marduk for his glory, calling upon him by his many names: Wise in Counsel, Great Provider, Lord of Life, Creator of All Things, and many other great names besides, all the fifty names of the great god Marduk, the mighty one and hero, who made the heavens and the Earth, who set the gods in their abodes, and who made human beings to be their servants.

Atrahasis

Many cultures have narratives of a great flood that wipes away all life with the exception of a few righteous survivors, and ancient Mesopotamian culture was no different. There are several different versions of the Flood narrative in both Sumerian and Akkadian; one such survives within the context of the Gilgamesh epic. The retelling presented below is based on the Old Babylonian version, which dates from the 17th century BCE, according to Benjamin Foster in his translation of the tale.

In the beginning of the world, there were no people. Only the gods walked the Earth, and the gods themselves had to work for their sustenance. The Annunaki themselves, the greater gods, had to dig the canals, till the fields, tend the beasts, and bring in the harvests.

"This work is too much," said the Annunaki. "Our backs bend under this heavy load. We must get someone else to do this for us."

And so the Annunaki decided that they would go up into the sky. First they cast lots to see where they would go. Anu the Father of All went up into the sky. Ellil took the Earth for his domain, and Enki took the sea. Then the Annunaki made the Igigi, the lesser gods, do all of the work that they had formerly done. They made the Igigi dig the canals, till the fields, tend the beasts, and bring in the harvests.

The first deed of the Igigi was to dig the riverbed for the Tigris. Then they dug the bed for the Euphrates. They set up the Apsu, the home of the gods, on their lands. For forty years, the Igigi labored at the Annunaki's command, and finally they had had enough of it. "Let us go to Ellil and throw him down. We will throw him down from his seat, and he will no longer have dominion over us. We will bring battle to his gates and overthrow him, and then we will be free!"

The Igigi made a great pyre of their work tools and set it ablaze. Then they took up their weapons, and in the middle of the night they marched on the E-kur, the house of Ellil. Ellil did not know of the approach of the Igigi, but Kalkal, a servant of Ellil, had done his duty well and had barred the gates of the E-kur long since. Kalkal saw the approach of the Igigi. He went to Nusku, another servant of Ellil, and told him, "Go to our master. Rouse him. Let him know that a great mob is approaching the E-kur. They will surround us. Tell Ellil, quickly!"

Nusku ran to Ellil's chamber and told him about the mob that was surrounding the E-kur. "Take up weapons!" said Ellil. "Take up your weapons, and stand in front of me. Bar the door to my chamber, but you stand between it and me, with your weapons at the ready!"

Nusku looked at Ellil and said, "O my master, why are you so pale? What is it you fear from those who are outside our walls? If you are so afraid, summon Anu to your aid! Summon Enki to your aid! Surely they will help you."

Ellil summoned Anu, and he summoned Enki. Anu said, "What is it? Why do you summon us?"

Ellil said, "Look about you! Look how the rabble surround my home! Look how they pound at my gates! What am I to do about this? These are my own children, risen up against me! My own children have taken up weapons, and they have laid siege to my home."

"Do you know what it is they want?" said Anu. "Why are they here? Maybe you should find that out first. Send Nusku out to them. Have Nusku ask them what they want of you and why they have taken up weapons against you. Send him in the name of the Annunaki."

Nusku went to the gate. He opened it and stood before the Igigi. He bowed to them and said, "I am here in the name of Anu, your father; and of Ellil, warrior and counsellor; and of Ninurta, your chamberlain; and of Ennugi, who controls the canals. I am here in their name to ask you why you are here and what you want. Who started this? Who decided that you should take up weapons and surround the house of Ellil? Speak! Tell me why you are here."

The Igigi answered, one and all, "Together we decided to take up weapons. Together we decided to lay siege to the house of Ellil. The Annunaki set us to work for them. Hard and long has been our labor. Our backs are bent, and our bodies are weary. We have had enough! And so we bring battle to the gates of the E-kur. We will fight for our freedom!"

Nusku went back to Ellil and told him what the Igigi had said. Ellil wept when he heard the plight of the Igigi. "O father Anu," he said, "can nothing be done to help my children? Can nothing be done to ease their burdens?"

Anu summoned together the council of the Annunaki, that they might discover what ought to be done about the plight of the Igigi. Enki spoke before the council, saying, "Yes, we ought to help the Igigi. Truly we gave them a burden that is too heavy for them. I know what we ought to do. We should create human beings. We should create them and give the labor of the Igigi to them." Enki turned to Mami, the mother-goddess, and said, "O Mami, could you create human beings? Could you make them, so that we might give to them the labor of the Igigi?"

But Mami replied, "This is not for me to do. You must be the one to create the humans. But if you give me clay, I will shape them."

"Very well," said Enki. "This is what I shall do: I will make a bath of purification on the first, seventh, and fifteenth days of the month, so that the gods might be purified. One god shall we sacrifice, and his blood will be mixed with Mami's clay."

And so this was done. The Annunaki made the purification baths, and they sacrificed Aw-ila, who gave himself for this purpose. Mami took the clay and mixed it with Aw-ila's blood, and so it was that the human being had also a spirit, because it was made with the blood of a god.

When the clay was well mixed with the blood, Enki called together the whole assembly of the gods. The Annunaki came at Enki's summons, and they spat upon the clay. The Igigi came at Enki's summons, and they spat upon the clay. Then Mami said to the whole assembly, "I have completed the task that you set me. Here is the clay that has the blood and the spirit of a god. From this, I will make beings to take upon them your labor and your pain. Before you is the beginning of new creatures, creatures who also may bewail their lot, who also may weary our ears with their clamoring."

Hearing this, the Igigi surged forward and fell at Mami's feet. They kissed her feet, saying, "We called you Mami, but now you shall be known as Mistress of All the Gods."

Enki and Mami summoned fourteen goddesses who would bear the new beings. While Enki trod the clay, kneading it with his feet, Mami said an incantation. When the clay was well mixed and the incantation done, Mami divided the clay into fourteen portions. Seven pieces she set on the right, and seven she set on the left. Seven pieces of clay were given to seven of the goddesses, and the beings they bore became males. The other seven pieces of clay were given to the other seven goddesses, and the beings they bore became females.

Mami told the new beings that they should each choose another to be their mate, one male with one female. She instructed them on how to live, and how they would bear their children, and on the proper reverence to the gods.

And so it was that the new men and women were put upon the Earth, and to them was given the labor that the gods had done. The new men and women dug the canals, tilled the fields, tended the beasts, and brought in the harvests. The new men and women did this labor, and they also married and had many fine children.

Twelve hundred years went by. The new human beings did their labor, and they had their children, and their children had children, and on and on this went until the Earth was well covered with human beings, and the noise of their clamoring rose up into the heavens, offending the ears of the gods.

"Oh!" cried Ellil. "This cannot stand. The noise of these beings is too much. I cannot sleep because of their din. We should diminish them. Let us make a plague, and send it upon them. Let us send a plague to kill them and diminish their numbers, and diminish their noise thereby."

The other gods readily agreed to this. "Yes, let us send a plague. Truly there are too many people, and truly they make such a din that none of us can sleep. Let us send a plague!"

And so the gods sent a plague upon the people. The plague swept through the land, and many died. Men, women, and children, young and old, all fell victim. One among them who survived was a wise man named Atrahasis. He was a devout man, speaking often with the god Enki. In turn, Enki honored Atrahasis by speaking with him.

"O Enki!" cried Atrahasis. "How long must we suffer like this? How long will the gods afflict us with this plague? Our children are dying, and our elders. Wives are leaving their husbands widowers, and husbands widow their wives. Help us! What can we do to appease the gods?"

"Call together the council of elders," said Enki. "Call them together, and tell them that they must all forgo the worship of their own gods.

Instead, they must build a temple for Namtar, god of plagues. For him must they bake bread, and to his temple must they bring it. When he sees the fine gift of bread laid at his door, perhaps he will feel ashamed and stop the plague."

Atrahasis did as Enki instructed. He told the elders what must be done. Together the people built a great temple to Namtar. They baked bread for him and laid it at the door of the temple. Namtar smelled the perfume of the baking bread. He saw how well crafted the loaves were and how many had been laid at the door of his temple. He felt ashamed for having afflicted the people, and so he withdrew the plague from them. Those who had been stricken began to get well again, and no one else fell ill.

Twelve hundred years went by after the end of the plague. The people did their labor, and they had their children, and their children had children, and on and on this went until the Earth was well covered with human beings, and the noise of their clamoring rose up into the heavens, offending the ears of the gods.

"Oh!" cried Ellil. "This cannot stand. The noise of these beings is too much. I cannot sleep because of their din. We should diminish them. Let us make a drought, and send it upon them. Let us send a drought so that their crops will not flourish. They will starve, and diminish their numbers, and diminish their noise thereby."

The other gods readily agreed to this. "Yes, let us send a drought. Truly there are too many people, and truly they make such a din that none of us can sleep. Let us send a drought!"

The gods called upon Adad, god of rain. "Stop the rain, Adad," said the gods. "Stop the rain so that the Earth dries up, so that the crops will not grow. That way the people will starve, and they will die, and finally it will be quiet enough for us to sleep."

And so Adad held back the rain. Drought came upon the land. The crops dried up, and the people thirsted, and soon many and many died.

The wise man Atrahasis again went to Enki and said, "How long must we suffer like this? How long will the gods afflict us with this drought? Our children are dying, and our elders. Wives are leaving their husbands widowers, and husbands widow their wives. Help us! What can we do to appease the gods?"

"Call together the council of elders," said Enki. "Call them together, and tell them that they must all forgo the worship of their own gods. Instead, they must build a temple for Adad, the rain-god. For him must they bake bread, and to his temple must they bring it. When he sees the fine gift of bread laid at his door, perhaps he will feel ashamed and stop the drought."

Atrahasis did as Enki instructed. He told the elders what must be done. Together the people built a great temple to Adad. They baked bread for him and laid it at the door of the temple. Adad smelled the perfume of the baking bread. He saw how well crafted the loaves were and how many had been laid at the door of his temple. He felt ashamed for having afflicted the people, and so he withdrew the drought from them. He gave them rain in plenty and morning dew. Soon the fields were bearing crops, and there was a plentiful harvest. Hunger and thirst were gone from the land.

Again the people became too noisy for the gods, and again the gods sent plague upon them. Again the gods sent plague, and when the numbers of the people were reduced, the gods relented.

After the plague was banished from the land, the people increased, and once again they disturbed the gods with their noise and bustle. Again the gods sent drought, and when the numbers of the people were reduced, the gods relented.

Twice the gods sent plague and then removed it. Twice the gods sent drought and then removed it. But after every plague and drought abated, the people increased their numbers until the din of their living echoed through the House of the Gods and the gods could no longer sleep.

Finally Ellil called together the Annunaki. He called them to a council and said, "Something must be done about the racket the people make. They are so noisy, none of us can sleep! We have tried plague. We have tried drought. Neither of those worked for long. We must do something more, something that will wipe out the people, so that we can sleep. I wish to bring a great flood upon the land. That will wipe out all the people, and at last we shall have peace."

Enki stood in council and cried out against this plan. "This is an evil thing you do, Ellil! Why should we wipe out all the people? Why should I desire to slay all of my children? Do this deed if you must, but I will have no part of it!"

And so Enki resolved to save at least some of the people from the wrath of Ellil and the Annunaki. Enki went to the wise man Atrahasis and sent to him a dream. Enki came to Atrahasis at night while he was sleeping, and he said, "Atrahasis! A great flood is coming, one that will wipe out every living thing. But I, Enki, your god, command you. Make a boat. Build it well, and seal it with pitch. Build it with many decks. Build it long, and build it wide. Take with you on your boat as many living things as you can. Seven days have you, before the flood arrives. Go and do my bidding, if you would live!"

Atrahasis woke from his dream. He straightway began building his boat, and his family helped him. Soon the great boat was built and provisioned, and Atrahasis filled it with the animals as Enki had commanded him to do. When the boat was ready, Atrahasis brought his family aboard. They sat down to a meal together, but Atrahasis was restless. He could not sit still. He could not eat or drink. He kept going outside and looking to see whether the flood was coming. Although he had built the boat that would save him, his heart was wretched, and he was sore afraid.

Atrahasis watched the skies. As he watched them, they grew dark with clouds, darker than Atrahasis had ever seen. Adad rode in those clouds, and he unleashed their rains upon the earth. Atrahasis went back into his boat and sealed up the doors with pitch.

The Anzu Bird roared through the sky. He rent the sky with his talons. And then it was that the flood came forth. It rushed out over the land in a great wall, washing away everything in its path. So great was the deluge that even the gods became frightened and hid within the walls of their House. Enki wailed in mourning for the death of all his children.

The entire world was scoured clean by the flood, and soon the Annunaki and the Igigi became hungry. They became hungry because the flood had washed away everything. All the people were dead, and all the fields lay under a great depth of water. The great mother-goddess Mami lamented the destruction. "O that the day may never again break! Woe to me that I agreed to Ellil's chosen path! Would that Anu had intervened and checked Ellil's course as he ought to have done!"

Ellil looked out over what he had wrought, thinking that finally he would have peace. But then he spied the boat of Atrahasis, and he fell into a rage. "Look at that! Look, out on the water! There is a boat, and it is filled with people and animals! We gods agreed together that all living things were to be destroyed. We gods agreed together that nothing should survive this flood. Only Enki could have done this thing. Only Enki would dare go against the will of all the gods!"

"Yes, I did this thing," said Enki. "And I would do it again, a thousand times over. My work it is to see that life is protected. The flood was an evil deed, Ellil, for you have punished the just along with the unjust."

[The remainder of the tale is fragmentary, but apparently Enki and Nintu, the goddess of giving birth, work together to create new people and establish a new social order. One remaining fragment deals with assigning roles to women as the bearers of children and priestesses who are to remain childless.]

Etana

This story is set in Kish, which was an ancient Sumerian city-state in what is now Iraq, and is about Etana, who the story says was the first king of Kish. However, the Sumerian King List puts Etana as the thirteenth king of Kish, so it is possible that one purpose of this story was to bolster Etana's historical clout and claim to authority.

One important theme of this story is the relationship between parents and children. Etana has no children of his own, and this is a sorrow to him; part of the story deals with his attempts to get an heir. The two other main characters in the story are an eagle and a serpent, both of which have broods that they are raising. The eagle's youngest chick attempts to advise his parent, while the serpent's children all fall prey to the greedy eagle. The serpent duly punishes the eagle for his treachery, but the eagle's redemption is found when he assists Etana to get the plant that will allow him to have children of his own.

In the beginning, the gods created the Earth and filled it with people. The gods also created a great city, the city of Kish. The Annunaki laid the plans for the city, and the Igigi built it from good brick. When the city was built, the gods decreed a great feast for all the people, but the gods would not let them into the city for the people had no king to rule them and to establish order. The gods searched all the lands for a man to be king over the city and finally declared that Etana should be made king in Kish.

In thanksgiving for his kingship, Etana built a shrine to the rain-god Adad, whom Etana especially revered. Next to the shrine, Etana planted a poplar tree, and when it came into its growth, an eagle made its eyrie in the branches, and a serpent made its burrow in the roots. The eagle said to the serpent, "We are neighbors here, so let us also be friends."

The serpent replied, "This I cannot do, for you have transgressed against Shamash, the god of the sun. But if you will swear with me not to overstep the limits of Shamash, then we can be companions.

Let us swear that whoever oversteps the limits of Shamash receive a great punishment."

The eagle agreed to this, and so they both swore on the Underworld not to anger Shamash. The serpent and the eagle then worked together, taking it in turns to find prey and bring it back to their homes. When it was the eagle's day to hunt, he would find wild oxen and wild asses and bring them back to the tree, and the serpent and his children would eat of what the eagle brought. When it was the serpent's day to hunt, he would bring back deer and gazelles, and the eagle and his children would eat of what the serpent brought.

For a time, the eagle and the serpent lived in peace together, hunting their prey and feeding one another's children. But soon the eagle began to think ill of the serpent. He plotted in his heart to eat the serpent's children. The eagle said to his brood, "I have a mind to eat the serpent's children. Then the serpent will run away, and we shall have the whole tree to ourselves."

The smallest chick said to his father, "No, Father! This is an evil thought. You must not eat the serpent's children, for you swore an oath to Shamash to live in peace with the serpent. If you eat the serpent's children, surely Shamash will punish you most sorely!"

But the eagle did not listen to the words of the youngest chick. He waited until the serpent had gone out to hunt, and then he flew down to the roots of the tree and ate up all the young serpents. That evening, when the serpent returned with its kill, he looked in his burrow and found it empty. He looked at the ground outside the burrow and saw it scored with the marks of the eagle's talons.

The serpent mourned deeply. He wept bitter tears, mourning for his dead children. Then the serpent turned his eyes to the heavens and said, "O Shamash, look what has become of my family! I trusted the eagle, and we swore an oath together. I trusted him, and together we worked to feed our young. But the eagle has betrayed me. He has devoured all my children. They are dead and gone, but his fledglings grow and flourish. O Shamash, I ask you to take vengeance on the eagle for this deed and for breaking his solemn oath to you!"

Shamash saw the tears of the serpent and heard his words. He said, "This is what you shall do. Go out hunting. Find a fine wild ox, and kill it. When it is dead, cut open its belly, and hide yourself in its entrails. Soon the birds will see the dead ox and will come down to feast upon it, and the eagle will come down with them. When the eagle begins to eat of the entrails, seize him, cut off his wings, and pluck out his tail feathers. Then cast him into a pit, and leave him there to die of hunger and thirst."

The serpent did as Shamash commanded. He slew the ox and hid himself in the beast's entrails. The eagle saw the dead ox and said to his children, "Come, let us feast! There is a fine dead ox there, and we shall eat well!"

But the smallest chick said, "No, Father! You must not eat of that ox. What if the serpent is hiding inside it? Surely he is wroth that you devoured his young. He may have set a trap for you!"

The eagle did not listen to his chick. He flew down to the dead ox and began walking around it and on top of it, trying to find which was the best part to eat first. The eagle decided to go for the entrails, but when he was close enough, the serpent darted out from his covert and seized the eagle's wings.

"You invaded my burrow! You devoured my young!" shouted the serpent.

In great fear, the eagle cried, "Have mercy! Do not hurt me! If you let me go unharmed, I will reward you greatly!"

"I cannot let you go," said the serpent, "for in capturing you, I am following the command of Shamash himself, and if I do not do what he commands, I shall be punished. But I have done no wrong and deserve no punishment, while you have devoured my children and must pay for that deed!"

And so, the serpent cut off the eagle's wings and plucked out his tail feathers, then cast him into a pit and left him there to die. Every day, the eagle called to Shamash, saying, "Do not leave me here! Do not let me die in a pit! If you save me, I shall see to it that your name receives praise from every tongue of every creature!"

Shamash replied, "Why should I save you? You did a most evil thing. You devoured the serpent's children, and you broke the solemn oath you swore to me. I will not help you, but perhaps a mortal man will."

Now, at this time, Etana ruled over the city of Kish, and he had but one sorrow: he had no children of his own. Every day, Etana prayed to Shamash, saying, "O Shamash, listen to my prayer! I have fed you on the finest beasts of my flocks. I have poured the blood of my sacrifices out so that the Underworld might drink of it. I honor all the gods, and try to do right, but still I have no children. Mighty Shamash, I beg of you, reveal to me how I might have children. Reveal to me how I might get an heir. Show me where grows the plant of birth!"

Shamash heard the prayers of Etana and said to him, "Follow the road that leads into the mountains. You will find there a pit, and in the pit is an eagle. The eagle will show you where the plant is."

Etana did as Shamash commanded. He followed the road that led into the mountains, and there he found the pit. The eagle heard Etana's approach, and he cried out to Shamash, saying, "O mighty Shamash! Is this the man you promised would help me? Give to him the gift of understanding birds' speech, and let me understand his!"

Shamash did as the eagle asked. He gave the eagle the power to understand Etana's speech and gave Etana the power to understand what the eagle said. The eagle cried out from the bottom of the pit, "Tell me why you are here!"

"I am looking for the plant of birth," said Etana. "Mighty Shamash told me to come here. He said you would be able to help me. I am a king, but I have no heir, and it is a great sorrow to me."

"Help me," said the eagle, "and I will show you where the plant grows."

And so Etana helped the eagle. Every day, he brought food for the bird to eat, until its wings healed and its tail feathers grew back. Etana fed the eagle and taught it to fly again. For seven months, Etana fed the eagle and taught it to fly, and when the seven months were over, Etana helped the eagle out of the pit.

After Etana cared for him, the eagle was well and strong again. "I thank you for your help," said the eagle. "Tell me, how I may serve you, in return for your kindness?"

"Find for me the plant of birth that I might have an heir," said Etana.

The eagle flew up into the sky. He flew all around, but the plant was nowhere to be found. The eagle returned to Etana and said, "Maybe it would be better if you helped me search. Here, climb up on my back. We shall fly together, and search together. We shall go to Ishtar, the goddess of birth. Perhaps she will tell us where the plant is."

Etana mounted the back of the eagle. The eagle took flight, and when they were high in the sky, he cried out to Etana, "Look how small the Earth seems from up here! Look how small the sea appears!"

Higher and higher they flew, and the land and sea looked smaller and smaller, until finally they were so high that Etana could no longer see either the land or the sea, and he became very frightened indeed.

"My friend, set me down!" said Etana. "I do not wish to fly all the way up to heaven. Set me down, and let me return home to my city!"

The eagle dropped Etana off his back. Etana fell down one league, but then the eagle caught him with his wings. Then the eagle dropped Etana again and caught him again a league farther down. Once more the eagle dropped Etana and caught him when Etana was barely three cubits above the ground.

[Here there is a gap in the narrative. The story resumes with Etana telling the eagle about a dream he had.]

Etana said to the eagle, "My friend, I had a great dream last night. Surely it was sent by the gods. Let me tell you what happened. Together we went up to heaven, you and I. We came to the House of the Gods. First we went through the gates of Anu, Ellil, and Ea. Then we went through the gates of Sin, Shamash, Adad, and Ishtar. We bowed low before the gods, both you and I. After we passed through all the gates, we saw a house before us. We went into the house, and there was seated the most beautiful woman. She wore upon her head a shining crown. Also in the house was a finely carved throne, and under the throne there were three lions. I stepped toward the throne, but the lions sprang at me, and I woke up, shivering with fear."

"Oh!" said the eagle. "I know what this means. I must take you up to heaven. Climb on my back, and we will fly there together."

Etana mounted the back of the eagle. The eagle took flight, and when they were high in the sky, he cried out to Etana, "Look how small the Earth seems from up here! Look how small the sea appears!"

Higher and higher they flew, and the land and sea looked smaller and smaller, until finally they were so high that Etana could no longer see either the land or the sea. Higher and yet higher they flew until they arrived in heaven at the House of the Gods. Together Etana and the eagle went through the gates of Anu, Ellil, and Ea. Then they went through the gates of Sin, Shamash, Adad, and Ishtar. They bowed low before the gods together. After they passed through all the gates, they saw before them a house. They opened the door and went inside.

[The remainder of the story is missing, with the exception of a fragment that indicates Etana was able to obtain the plant of birth and return home with it.]

Part II: Tales of Gods and Goddesses

Ishtar Descends to the Underworld

This story explains what happens when the goddess Ishtar decides to pay a visit to the Underworld, which is ruled by Ereshkigal, her older sister and a rival goddess. It is somewhat unclear what Ishtar intends to accomplish by her visit, but Ereshkigal seems to be under the impression that Ishtar intends to supplant her. Ereshkigal therefore acts accordingly to strip Ishtar of her power by taking Ishtar's clothing and jewelry, piece by piece, so that the goddess must enter the Underworld as the human dead do, naked and alone.

Ishtar is a fertility goddess; when she is imprisoned by Ereshkigal, no procreation can take place upon the earth. The god Ea creates a beautiful eunuch named Asushunamir (although some translators state that this character may have been a male prostitute or transvestite) to trick Ereshkigal into letting Ishtar return to the world of the living. Assyriologist Benjamin R. Foster, in his translation of the story, notes that sending such a person would have been seen by Mesopotamian peoples as apropos, since Ishtar was the patron goddess of male prostitutes and transvestites, who worked as entertainers, and it is in this capacity that the eunuch enters the Underworld to trick Ereshkigal.

Two portions of the story seem to be omitted in the Akkadian version, and have been supplied from Foster's notes on the tale. These have to do with Asushunamir's interaction with Ereshkigal and with the reason why Tammuz is sent to the Underworld when Ishtar returns to the world of the living.

There came a time when the goddess Ishtar, daughter of the moon-god Sin, determined to go to the Underworld. She went to the Underworld, the place all enter but none leave, the place at which all roads end, a lightless place, and those who dwell therein eat clay and drink dust.

Ishtar went to the gates of the Underworld and said, "Gatekeeper, open the gate! Open for me, lest I break down these doors. Open for me, lest I raise the dead so that they might feed upon the living, and soon more shall be dead than alive. Open the gate!"

The gatekeeper said, "O Lady Ishtar, have patience, and wait a while. I must ask permission of my Lady Ereshkigal before opening to anyone, even to the Lady Ishtar."

The gatekeeper went to Ereshkigal and said, "O Lady Ereshkigal, your sister Ishtar waits at the gate of the Underworld and demands I open to her. The one who stirs up the deep in the sight of Ea is here and craves admittance."

Ereshkigal paled when she heard the gatekeeper's speech. "What might Ishtar hold against me that she visits me here? Shall I join the ones whose road has ended here? Shall I dwell in the place all enter but none leave? Shall I eat clay and drink dust? Shall I mourn for the young men torn from their brides and for the young women torn from their grooms? Shall I mourn for the stillborn and the infants who had so little of life?"

Then Ereshkigal said to the gatekeeper, "Ishtar may enter, but see to it she obeys the ancient laws."

The gatekeeper returned to the gate and said to Ishtar, "You may enter, Lady Ishtar. Enter and let the Underworld rejoice at your arrival."

The gatekeeper took Ishtar to the first gate. There he took from Ishtar her great crown and opened for her the gate.

"Why do you take from me my crown?" said Ishtar.

"I bid you enter, my lady," said the gatekeeper. "I take the crown because it is an ancient law of this place, and I must uphold it."

The gatekeeper took Ishtar to the second gate. There he took from Ishtar her earrings.

"Why do you take from me my earrings?" said Ishtar.

"I bid you enter, my lady," said the gatekeeper. "I take the earrings because it is an ancient law of this place, and I must uphold it."

The gatekeeper took Ishtar to the third gate. There he took from Ishtar her necklace of beads.

"Why do you take from me my necklace of beads?" said Ishtar.

"I bid you enter, my lady," said the gatekeeper. "I take the necklace of beads because it is an ancient law of this place, and I must uphold it."

The gatekeeper took Ishtar to the fourth gate. There he took from Ishtar the fastenings of her garment.

"Why do you take from me the fastenings of my garment?" said Ishtar

"I bid you enter, my lady," said the gatekeeper. "I take the fastenings of your garment because it is an ancient law of this place, and I must uphold it."

The gatekeeper took Ishtar to the fifth gate. There he took from Ishtar the belt decked with birthstones.

"Why do you take from me my belt decked with birthstones?" said Ishtar.

"I bid you enter, my lady," said the gatekeeper. "I take the belt decked with birthstones because it is an ancient law of this place, and I must uphold it."

The gatekeeper took Ishtar to the sixth gate. There he took from Ishtar the bracelets from her wrists and the anklets from her feet.

"Why do you take from me my bracelets from my wrists and the anklets from my feet?" said Ishtar.

"I bid you enter, my lady," said the gatekeeper. "I take the bracelets from your wrists and the anklets from your feet because it is an ancient law of this place, and I must uphold it."

The gatekeeper took Ishtar to the seventh gate. There he took from Ishtar the garment of her body.

"Why do you take from me the garment of my body?" said Ishtar.

"I bid you enter, my lady," said the gatekeeper. "I take the garment of your body because it is an ancient law of this place, and I must uphold it."

Ishtar entered the presence of Ereshkigal, who trembled with anger. Not waiting for Ereshkigal to speak, Ishtar approached her.

Ereshkigal cried out, "Namtar, my wise counsellor! Take Ishtar away from me at once! Let her be riddled with diseases of all kinds, diseases of her eyes and skin, diseases of her hands and feet, diseases of her heart and head. Take her away, and strike her thus!"

And so it was that Ishtar was held in the Underworld, cursed by Ereshkigal. And upon the earth, the bull would not mount the cow. The young groom did not lie down with his bride. The husband slept in one room, and the wife in another.

Papsukkal, the wise counsellor of the Annunaki, saw what happened upon the Earth, and he was greatly saddened. He cast himself into mourning, donning ragged garments and letting his hair go unkempt. In mourning, Papsukkal went before Ea and said, "The Lady Ishtar has gone into the Underworld, and all is awry. The bull will not mount the cow. The young groom will not lie with his bride. The husband sleeps in one room, and the wife in another."

Ea heard the words of Papsukkal and saw his grief. Ea therefore created Asushunamir, a eunuch of great beauty. Ea said to Asushunamir, "Go down to the Underworld. Go to the Lady Ereshkigal. She will be entranced by you. When her anger is appeased, ask her to swear by the Annunaki, and then ask her to give you the waterskin that you might drink."

Asushunamir did as Ea instructed, but when he asked for the waterskin, Ereshkigal became enraged. "How dare you ask this thing! You have no right. A curse be upon you! You shall beg crusts from the bakers of the city, and drink from the public sewer. You shall stand only in the shadows, and you shall dwell only within doorways. Drunk and sober alike shall strike you in the face."

Then Ereshkigal said to Namtar, "Go to the E-galgina, the Eternal Palace. Decorate the doorways with coral and fine shells. Bring forth the Annunaki, let them be seated upon golden thrones. Take up the Water of Life, and sprinkle it upon Ishtar. Then take her away from here, out of the Underworld."

Namtar did as Ereshkigal commanded. He decorated the doorways of the E-galgina with coral and fine shells. He brought forth the Annunaki and seated them upon golden thrones. He took up the Water of Life and sprinkled it upon Ishtar. Then he brought her to the gates.

At the first gate, he returned to Ishtar the garment of her body and let her out the gate.

At the second gate, he returned to Ishtar the bracelets of her wrists and the anklets of her feet and let her out the gate.

At the third gate, he returned to Ishtar the belt of birthstones and let her out the gate.

At the fourth gate, he returned to Ishtar the fastenings of her garment and let her out the gate.

At the fifth gate, he returned to Ishtar her necklace of beads and let her out the gate.

At the sixth gate, he returned to Ishtar her earrings and let her out the gate.

At the seventh gate, he returned to Ishtar her great crown and let her out the gate.

Ereshkigal also said to Namtar, "If Ishtar does not pay her ransom price, you are to return her to the Underworld. When you let her go, bring here Tammuz, her lover. Bathe him in clearest water, and anoint him with fragrant oil. Dress him in fine red clothing, and give him a flute of lapis to play music upon and a ring of carnelian to adorn his finger. Send prostitutes to him that he might delight in them."

Ishtar rose up from the Underworld and found Tammuz at his ease, playing music on his flute and delighting in prostitutes. "What is this that you do?" she said. "Why do you not hold yourself in mourning, seeing that I was held captive in the Underworld?"

Then Ishtar cursed Tammuz, saying, "May the Lady Ereshkigal take you in my stead!"

Belili, the sister of Tammuz, was adorning herself with jewelry when the wail for Tammuz went up. She cast aside her jewels and cried out, "Do not take from me my brother! On the day when Tammuz returns, the lapis flute and carnelian ring will rejoice. Those who wail and keen will rejoice, and the dead shall smell the incense."

Nergal and Ereshkigal

Two versions of this myth exist. The earlier version, which was found in Tell el-Amarna, Egypt, appears to date from the 15th or 14th

centuries BCE. This version is relatively short and involves the god Nergal's hostile takeover of the Underworld with the help of a company of demons. One important function of this version of the text seems to have been to help ancient Egyptian scribes learn Akkadian.

In the longer, later, Babylonian version, Nergal receives special instructions from Ea about how to behave so as not to become captive in the Underworld, including the command not to give in to any desire he may have for Ereshkigal, the goddess of the Underworld, no matter how she might tempt him. Of course, Nergal follows all of Ea's commandments except the one about desire, and he eventually assumes the throne of the Underworld by becoming Ereshkigal's lover. It is the second, longer version that is presented here, although the ending has sadly been lost.

There came a time when the gods decided to hold a great feast, and so they sent a messenger to the Underworld to the goddess Ereshkigal, where she dwelled in her domain. The messenger said to Ereshkigal, "The gods, my masters, bid me to tell you that they are having a great feast. You cannot go up to their domain, and they may not come down to yours, so send a servant up to the gods so that the servant might bring you your share of the feast."

Ereshkigal called to herself her chief counsellor, Namtar. "Go up to where the gods are having their feast," said Ereshkigal. "Greet my fellow gods well, and bring back to me my portion."

Namtar went to the dwelling of the gods where they sat at their feast. When Namtar entered the banqueting chamber, the gods rose to greet him. One god, however, remained seated: Nergal. He refused to do honor to the chief counsellor of the goddess of the Underworld.

When Namtar returned to the Underworld with Ereshkigal's portion of the feast, he told her what had happened and how Nergal had refused to stand to honor him as the messenger of the goddess. Ereshkigal was greatly affronted. "Go back to the domain of the gods. Go thither, and bring back to me the one who did not honor you that I may kill him!"

Namtar went back to the domain of the gods. He said to them, "When I came to get Ereshkigal's portion of the feast, there was one among you who did not stand to greet me. I am commanded to bring him back with me so that he might answer for his insolence."

Namtar looked all around the hall, but he did not see Nergal among the other gods, for Nergal was greatly afraid, and he had crouched down behind the others so that Namtar might not see him.

Then Namtar went back to Ereshkigal and said, "I went to the domain of the gods. I looked for the one who slighted me, but he was not there."

"Go back to the domain of the gods," said Ereshkigal, "and ask the help of our father Ea. Tell him that the one who did not rise to greet you must come to my domain to answer for his insolence."

And so a third time Namtar returned to the domain of the gods. He went before Ea and said, "Ereshkigal, my mistress, demands that you send the one who slighted me to the Underworld that he might pay for his insolence."

Ea agreed and then sent Namtar back to the Underworld to give Ereshkigal his word that Nergal would be sent. Then Ea caused Nergal to come before him. Nergal was greatly frightened, for he knew why Namtar had been sent.

"O Father Ea!" pleaded Nergal. "Do not send me away. Do not send me to the Underworld, for surely Ereshkigal will kill me!"

"Have no fear," said Ea. "You will be safe if you do as I instruct you. Make for yourself a chair. Bring it with you to the Underworld. When the people of the Underworld offer you a seat, do not take it. Sit in your own seat instead. If they offer you food or drink, you must refuse it. And if Ereshkigal should show you her body, you must refuse that as well."

Nergal took up his axe. He went and cut down trees to make his chair. He fashioned the chair well and decorated it brightly. This done, he set out for the Underworld.

After a long journey, he came to the gates of Ereshkigal's domain. Nergal knocked on the gates. A guardian looked through the peephole and said, "Who are you, and what is your errand here?"

"I am Nergal, and I am come in answer to Ereshkigal's summons."

"Wait here," said the guardian. "I must ask whether I am to allow you to enter."

The guardian went to fetch Namtar. "There is a god at the gate. He says he has come in answer to the Lady Ereshkigal's summons."

Namtar went to the gate. He looked through the peephole, and when he beheld Nergal standing there, waiting, he began shaking with rage. Namtar went to Ereshkigal and said, "The god who slighted me is here at the gate. What should be done with him?"

"It is not for you to deal out judgment to him," said Ereshkigal. "Bring him into my presence. I shall deal with him as I see fit."

Namtar went back to the gate and let Nergal in. Namtar led Nergal through all the seven gates of the Underworld, one by one, until they came to the courtyard of Ereshkigal. There Nergal threw himself at the feet of the goddess. "Our father Anu sent me to your realm" he said. "I am here and will do your bidding."

"Sit down on this throne," said Ereshkigal. "Sit down here on my throne and pronounce judgment."

But Namtar remembered the instructions of Ea, and he did not sit on Ereshkigal's throne. He sat on his own chair instead.

Ereshkigal commanded her servants to bring food and drink to her guest. The food and drink were set before Nergal, but he remembered the instructions of Ea, and he did not touch it.

Then Ereshkigal said, "It is time for me to go and bathe." She went to her bath, and she made sure that Nergal could see her as she removed her clothing. She made sure that Nergal could see her body.

When Nergal beheld how beautiful Ereshkigal was and how comely her body, he was overcome with desire for her. He went to her and embraced her. Together they went to her bed where they delighted in one another as men and women do. There they lay together for six days, delighting in one another.

On the seventh day, Nergal rose from Ereshkigal's bed. "I must leave you now," said Nergal, "but have no fear. I shall return to you."

Nergal went to the guardian of the gate, saying, "You must let me out! The goddess Ereshkigal has said that I am to be allowed to return to the domain of the gods."

The guardian let Nergal out. Nergal ascended to the domain of the gods. The gods saw him return and said, "Lo! Nergal has come back! Let Ea bless him with fresh water, and let him sit once more among us and eat our food and drink our drink." And so it was that Nergal rejoined the company of the gods in their domain, blinking at the drops of fresh water that Ea had sprinkled upon him.

Ereshkigal, for her part, did not know that Nergal had left the Underworld entirely. She called to her servants to sprinkle fresh water for him and to set out food and drink for him. But then Namtar came into her chamber, saying, "Nergal is not here! He has left the Underworld entirely and has returned to the domain of the gods!"

Ereshkigal cried out in despair. "Alas!" she cried. "Alas that Nergal has left me! My bed shall be cold. My nights shall be empty. Never again shall I know delight. Alas!"

Namtar said to Ereshkigal, "Let me return to the domain of the gods. Let me ask Anu and Ellil and Ea to let Nergal return to you."

"Yes, my wise counsellor," said Ereshkigal. "Yes, go back to the domain of the gods. Tell Anu and Ellil and Ea that they must return

Nergal to me. I feel a stirring in my belly; surely he has left me with child. Also, you must tell them that if Nergal is not returned to me, I shall raise all the dead. I shall raise the dead, and send them into the land of the living. The dead shall eat the living, and no one shall be left alive!"

Namtar went up to the domain of the gods. He went before Anu and Ellil and Ea, and told them what the goddess said. "Ereshkigal demands you return her lover to her. He has left her with child. She weeps over her cold and empty bed. She desires him to return. If he does not return, Ereshkigal shall raise the dead, and the dead shall eat the living until no one is left alive."

"Very well," said Ea. "Search for the one you want. See whether he is here among us."

Nergal went through the company of the gods. He looked this one in the face and that one, and when he came to a god whose head had been sprinkled with water, he did not recognize that it was Nergal.

Namtar therefore returned to the Underworld, and told Ereshkigal what had happened. "I went to the domain of the gods. I gave your message to Anu and Ellil and Ea. I looked through all the company of the gods, but I did not see the one you desired. I looked through all of them, even the one who was blinking from the water that had been sprinkled on his head."

"That is the one!" said Ereshkigal. "The one with the water on his head is the one I desire. Go back to the domain of the gods, and tell them they must send that one to me."

Namtar returned to the domain of the gods. Once again he went through their company, seeking the one he was to take back to Ereshkigal. Finally he found Nergal. Namtar said to him, "You must come back with me to the Underworld. Ereshkigal desires you and wishes you to come and live with her in her domain."

"Very well," said Nergal. "I shall come with you."

Then Namtar said, "Listen well to my instructions. At each gate, you must give something that belongs to you to the guardian who is there. But do not let the guardian take hold of you."

While Namtar went back to Ereshkigal's domain, Nergal made himself ready. He thought about the words of Namtar. He took up his bow and his arrows, and descended to the Underworld. When Nergal arrived at the first gate, he commanded the guardian to let him in. The guardian opened the gate, but before he could demand one of Nergal's belongings from him, before the guardian could take hold of Nergal, Nergal struck him down. Nergal went to the second gate, and there he struck down the guardian. Nergal went to the third gate and the fourth, and at each gate to the Underworld, he struck down the guardian.

Finally, Nergal arrived at the courtyard where Ereshkigal was. He ran up to her where she was seated on her throne. He took hold of her long hair and pulled her into an embrace. Passionately they embraced, and then they went to Ereshkigal's bed, where they delighted in one another once more. There they lay for the first day and the second day. They lay for the third, the fourth, the fifth, and the sixth day. And on the seventh day, Anu sent his messenger to Ereshkigal and Nergal, where they dwelled in the domain of the Underworld.

[*The remainder of the story has been lost.*]

Ninurta and the Anzu Bird

The Anzu Bird is a mythical creature that appears in both Sumerian and Akkadian stories. Having the head of a lion and the body of a bird, this fearsome beast was associated with thunder and could be either a good or an evil character depending on the story.

It is the evil character that comes to the fore in this story: the Anzu Bird is made guardian of the dwelling of the gods, and when he sees the Tablets of Destiny that are kept by Ellil, he is overcome with greed and lust for the power that the tablets represent. One day, when Ellil is taking a bath, the Anzu Bird steals the tablets and runs away to the mountains with them, throwing the universe into chaos because the seat of authority has been removed from Ellil and given to the capricious bird. When the Anzu Bird (or more simply, "Anzu") refuses to give the tablets back, the gods send the hero Ninurta to recover them. In a series of battles involving both martial skill and magic, Ninurta finally recovers the tablets and restores them to their rightful owner, which also restores order to the cosmos.

Ninurta himself is a god, the son of Ellil and the mother goddess Ninhursag. Ninurta had associations with both agriculture and lawgiving, and in both Sumerian and Akkadian tales he is the one hero the gods themselves turn to when a powerful enemy presents itself and must be destroyed.

In the time when the great Tigris and Euphrates had been made, their channels dug so that they might flow through the land but before they had been filled with water, and in the time before any places of honor had been built for the Igigi, the Younger Gods of Heaven, the great god Ellil came before the Igigi and said, "Lo! Upon the mountain there has come to be a great bird, the Anzu Bird, whose beak is like a saw. I do not know where Anzu comes from. Perhaps he was born out of the Earth herself. Perhaps he was born out of the stone of the mountain itself. I say we should bring the Anzu Bird here, to serve us. Let him guard our holy of holies."

And so it was that Anzu was brought to the Duranki, the dwelling of the gods, to watch over the holy of holies. Every day, Ellil would go into the sacred chamber and there bathe himself with holy water, and Anzu would watch over him while he bathed. Anzu looked upon lordly Ellil, his fine clothes, and his golden crown, but most of all, Anzu gazed upon the Tablets of Destiny, which were in Ellil's keeping. Anzu looked upon the Tablets, and within his heart formed a great desire to have them for himself.

"Oh, if only I could be the holder of the Tablets!" Anzu said to himself. "Then I would be first among all the gods. All would have to bow to me. All the Igigi would be in my thrall. Surely the Tablets shall be mine!"

Anzu waited until the next time Ellil went to the holy of holies to bathe in the sacred water. When Ellil had set aside his golden crown and his fine raiment, and when he had set aside the Tablets of Destiny and entered the sacred water, Anzu swooped down upon the Tablets. He took the Tablets of Destiny in his talons and flew away to the mountain where he had been born. Ellil watched Anzu take the Tablets. He watched Anzu fly away with the authority of the gods, leaving the dwelling of the Igigi without any of its power.

The gods gathered together to take counsel of one another as to what should be done. Soon enough it was decided that someone should climb the mountain, kill Anzu, and bring the Tablets back to their rightful owners.

First the gods turned to Adad, the son of Anu. "Go and kill Anzu," said the other gods. "You are strong and a brave warrior. You are the god of storms and rain. You control the water in the canals. You will have holy places throughout the world, and everyone will praise your name if you do this deed."

But Adad said, "The mountain is impassable. No one can climb it. Anzu has the Tablets of Destiny. All authority and power rests in him now. Surely if I try to take the Tablets away from him, he will destroy me. No, I shall not go. Find another to do this deed."

Then the Igigi turned to Erra, the son of Annunitum, and asked him to go kill Anzu and bring back the Tablets. But Erra gave the same answer as Adad; he would not go.

Next, the Igigi asked Shara, the son of Ishtar. "Go climb the mountain and kill Anzu," they said. "You are strong and a brave warrior. You are the god of war and the son of the goddess Ishtar.

You will have holy places throughout the world, and everyone will praise your name if you do this deed. Bring back the Tablets!"

But Shara gave the same answer as Adad and Erra. He would not go.

The gods grew vexed. They argued with one another. They blamed each other that no one would go climb the mountain. No one would kill the Anzu Bird and take back the Tablets. Everyone was too afraid of Anzu's power.

Ea stood aside from the other gods and their wrangling. He thought long and deep, and then he went to his father, Anu, and said, "Let me be the one to find a champion. Surely I can find someone who will go to the mountain to face Anzu and bring back the Tablets."

Anu thought this a good plan, and when Ea told the Igigi what he had in mind, they praised him loudly.

First, Ea had the gods summon to themselves the goddess Mami. They said to her, "O Divine Mistress, we have need of your aid. We need you to give us your beloved son, the strong and bold Ninurta, for surely only he can deliver us from our plight. We beg you to ask his help."

Mami went to her son and told him what Ea and the Igigi had said. "You must go to the mountain and kill Anzu. You must bring back the Tablets of Destiny. The halls of the gods have lost their luster, and there is no power or authority here anymore. Go climb the mountain. Take your mighty bow, and pierce him with arrows. Surround him with mists and fog so that he cannot see you. Shine as brightly as the sun so that he is blinded by you. Kill Anzu, and bring back the Tablets, and you shall have shrines built to you throughout the whole world."

Ninurta heeded the words of his mother. He armed himself and set out for the mountain. When Anzu saw Ninurta approaching, he became very angry. "How dare you come to face me? How dare you threaten the bearer of the Tablets of Destiny? I am now the authority! Mine is the power of the gods! Away with you!"

Ninurta answered, "I am Ninurta! I have come from the sacred Duranki, sent by the gods themselves. I have come to kill you and take back that which you have unlawfully stolen. Have at you, foul demon!"

Anzu raged at Ninurta's words. He covered the whole mountain with darkness. Shrieking, he descended upon the brave Ninurta, and together they battled up and down the mountainside. Long and hard they fought, and in the end, Ninurta's armor was all splashed with blood, but the Anzu Bird did not die.

Ninurta took his mighty bow and nocked an arrow to the string. He set the arrow in flight, aiming it at Anzu's heart. Anzu saw the arrow and said to it, "Arrow shaft! Return your cane to its riverside. Fletching! Return your feathers to their birds. Bow! Return your wood to its forest. String! Return your gut to its sheep."

And so it was that Ninurta's arrow could not approach Anzu. The arrow turned away and did the bird no harm, and no matter how Ninurta might try, he could not get the bow to draw with any power. The Anzu Bird had bewitched that mighty weapon, and it was of no aid to Ninurta now.

Ninurta called out for help. He called to the god Adad and said, "O Adad! Go you to our father Ea and tell him that I cannot kill the Anzu Bird. We fought, but I could not defeat him, and he has bewitched my mighty bow and my swift arrows so that they are of no help to me. Tell this to Ea, and then bring his answer back to me."

Adad did as Ninurta asked. He went to Ea and told of all that had happened on the mountain, of how Ninurta had not been able to kill the bird, and of how Anzu had enchanted Ninurta's bow and arrows.

Ea replied, "My son, do not be afraid! Do not cease in your efforts! You will be victorious. Attack the Anzu Bird. Attack him relentlessly. Attack him until he tires and can fight you no more. Fight him until all the feathers drop from his wings, and then cut them off with your sword. Anzu will try to reattach his wings, but never fear; once his feathers and wings are lost, he will not be able to withstand you. Call up the winds; bid them blow his feathers and wings away. Then you may take your mighty bow and launch a swift arrow at his breast. Grab Anzu by the neck, take your sword, and slit open his gullet!

"Do these things, and do them well. Return the Tablets of Destiny to their rightful owners. Restore order. Do these things, and you shall have many shrines and much honor, in heaven and on the Earth."

Adad returned to Ninurta and told him everything Ea had said. Ninurta hearkened well and girded himself once more for battle. He took up his mighty sword, the Seven of Battle. He called to himself the seven winds, they who create the dust storms. The winds he called to himself to be his army, and he arrayed them for war.

Again Ninurta advanced upon the Anzu Bird. Again their battle was fierce. But Ninurta did not cease to press his attack. On and on, he harried the great bird. On and on, Ninurta pressed him until Anzu began shedding the feathers of his wings in his weariness. When Ninurta saw this, he drew his sword and slashed off Anzu's wings. Anzu tried to reattach his wings. "Wing to wing!" he shouted, but before he could complete the spell, Ninurta nocked a swift arrow to his mighty bow and sent the dart deep into the breast of the Anzu Bird.

Ninurta did not cease his fighting once the bird was dead. First he went and slew the mountain. Ninurta slew the mountain that the Anzu Bird had defiled. Then he flooded the plains all around. With that done, Ninurta took up the Tablets of Destiny that Anzu had stolen and set out for the abode of the gods.

While Ninurta was still journeying back, an omen came to the Igigi. A great number of feathers floated into the abode of the gods, the feathers of the Anzu Bird. Dagan, god of the growing grain, saw the feathers. He called to all the other gods, saying, "Rejoice! Surely the hero Ninurta has slain the Anzu Bird and taken back the Tablets of

Destiny. See? Here are the feathers of the great bird, floating into our abode on the wind. Rejoice!"

Soon enough, the brave Ninurta returned, bearing the Tablets of Destiny in his powerful arms. Ninurta placed the tablets in the lap of Ellil, restoring them to their rightful owner, restoring order to all that is.

Ellil said, "Behold! The hero Ninurta has slain the Anzu Bird and restored the Tablets of Destiny! Let us praise his name henceforth, in heaven and upon the Earth. May he have many shrines and be called by many holy names. Praise to the hero Ninurta!"

Adapa and the South Wind

This brief story may appear relatively simple at first glance, but it contains a great deal of depth and complexity. The tale of Adapa is at once a trickster story, a tale of the relationship between mankind and divinity, a story about the fatal refusal of immortality made by a man who was supposedly divinely wise (or who perhaps wisely refused immortality), and a just-so fable about why human beings are both mortal and separated from the gods. Some scholars have seen antecedents for the Genesis tale of Adam and Eve in the Garden of Eden within the myth of Adapa, in that the gods make eternal life available to the protagonist(s), who ultimately do not achieve it.

However, the roles of food and obedience in the eventual outcome of each of these stories are different. In both stories, the main characters are told by a divine being not to eat what is made available to them. Adapa obeys the command of Ea not to eat the food of the gods, while Adam and Eve disobey and eat the forbidden fruit. Adapa is later chastised by the great god Anu for failing to eat the food of life, but Adam and Eve are exiled from paradise for taking the forbidden fruit.

Once there was a man named Adapa, who was favored of the gods and who was the son of the god Ea. The gods gave him great wisdom, wisdom like unto their own wisdom, but to Adapa, they did not grant eternal life.

Adapa lived in the city of Eridu, and to him Ea gave authority over all things so that he might pronounce judgment upon the people. A wise man was Adapa, and a pious one. He served in the temple, baking the sacred loaves, catching the sacred fish. Adapa it was who opened the temple doors, and Adapa it was who closed them again.

One day, Adapa went down to the harbor, for there was need of fish to feed the gods. Adapa went to the dock where his little fishing boat was moored. He got into the boat, and away he sailed. With the power given to him by the gods, he steered his boat out onto the open water, where he laid his nets for a catch of fish.

Having caught enough fish, Adapa made ready to return to the harbor. The sea had been calm and unruffled the whole day. Adapa's sailing and fishing had been easy and very pleasant. But when he tried to sail back to the harbor, the South Wind flew down upon him. So great was the power of the wind that Adapa's little boat was capsized, and all his catch was lost.

This made Adapa very angry. "May your wing break!" he said to the South Wind, and as soon as he said it, the South Wind's wing was broken. The South Wind could not blow from the sea onto the land. For seven days, there was no cooling wind from the sea. For seven days, the heat of the sun was not abated by a southerly sea breeze.

The god Anu suffered much from the heat. He called to himself Ilabrat, his messenger. "Tell me, Ilabrat," said Anu, "why is it that there is no good breeze from the sea? Where are the cooling winds?"

"O Anu," said Ilabrat, "it is because the man Adapa has broken the South Wind's wing. It cannot fly to bring the coolness from the sea onto the land."

"Oh!" cried Anu. "Oh, this is a great insult. Bring the man Adapa before me to answer for what he has done!"

Ea heard of Anu's anger toward Adapa. Ea went to his son and said, "You will be summoned before the god Anu for breaking the South Wind's wing. Dress yourself in ragged clothes. Leave your hair uncombed. Behave as though you are in deep mourning.

"When you arrive at the door to Anu's house, there will be two gods waiting there for you. These are Tammuz and Gizzida. They will ask you why you were mourning. You must tell them that you are mourning for two gods who have vanished. They will ask you which gods, and you must tell them 'Tammuz and Gizzida.' Then they will laugh in mirth at this, and bring you into Anu's presence. There they will speak a good word for you.

"Tammuz and Gizzida may offer you the food of death and the drink of death. Do not eat it! Do not drink it! But if they offer you clean clothing and oil to anoint your body, put on the clothing and anoint yourself with the oil. Do not forget what I have told you!"

Adapa did what Ea told him. He dressed himself in ragged clothes. He left his hair unkempt. He put on an air of mourning. And in this guise, he went to the gates of the house of Anu, where Tammuz and Gizzida were waiting outside the door.

When the two gods saw Adapa, they said, "Adapa! Whatever is the matter? Why do you go about in rags with your hair unkempt and an air of mourning about you?"

"Oh," said Adapa, "it is very sad indeed. Two gods have vanished! They have vanished and will never return, so I am mourning for them."

"Which gods are these?" asked Tammuz and Gizzida.

"Why, Tammuz and Gizzida, of course," replied Adapa. "They have vanished quite away. It is very sad."

Tammuz and Gizzida looked at one another and then began to laugh. They laughed for a very long time. But when they could catch their breaths again, they brought Adapa into the house of Anu to stand before Anu himself.

Anu said to Adapa, "Tell me, why did you break the South Wind's wing?"

Adapa said, "O Great Anu, I went fishing on the sea to get fish to feed the gods. When I had enough fish, I wanted to sail back to the harbor, but the South Wind flew down upon me and capsized my little boat. I lost all my catch. This made me very angry, so I cursed the South Wind, and now its wing is broken."

Anu began to be very angry indeed with Adapa, but Tammuz and Gizzida spoke on Adapa's behalf. They calmed the anger of Anu, just as Ea had said they would.

Anu sighed. "What did Ea think to accomplish by giving such power to a mere mortal? What should we do with this Adapa?"

Anu turned to his servants. "Bring this man the food of life. Bring this man the water of life. Bring him fresh clothing and oil with which to anoint himself."

The food and drink and clothing and oil were given to Adapa. Adapa put on the garment and anointed himself with the oil, but he did not touch either the food or the drink.

Anu wondered that Adapa would not eat or drink. "Adapa, surely you are hungry and thirsty. Why do you not eat? Why do you not drink? Do you not wish to live?"

"O Great Anu," said Adapa, "my father Ea told me, 'When you go to the house of Anu, you must not eat the food. You must not drink the water.' That is why I do not eat or drink."

Anu laughed. "Very well, suit yourself! Surely it is a strange thing that Ea should tell a mere mortal to disobey the commands of Anu."

Anu caused Adapa to be returned to his home in Eridu, where he became even more renowned for his wisdom and piety. But because Adapa had refused the food and water of life, he did not live forever. Only the memory of his wisdom and piety lived on, for Anu ordained it to be thus.

Part III: Selections from the *Epic of Gilgamesh*

The Epic of Gilgamesh *is one of the first tales of its kind ever recorded. It follows the friendship and adventures of Gilgamesh, king of Uruk, and his companion, Enkidu, a wild man created by the gods to curb Gilgamesh's excesses. These stories originated in Sumer as a loosely connected collection of tales about Gilgamesh and his friend, but the version presented below is based on the two most important later Akkadian versions: the Old Babylonian, which was compiled sometime around 1800 BCE, and the so-called Standard Version, which was compiled around 1200 BCE.*

The Akkadian versions of Gilgamesh's tale contain some of the same stories that the Sumerian version does, but they go far beyond the Sumerian version in terms of characterization. For example, the Akkadian versions of Gilgamesh *introduce Enkidu as a round character in his own right, explaining his backstory and telling how he and Gilgamesh came to be friends. Also enfolded into the Akkadian* Gilgamesh *is a version of the Sumerian Flood myth as told to Gilgamesh by Utnapishtim, the man who built the ark and survived that deluge and who was granted eternal life by the gods.*

But above all, the Babylonian Gilgamesh is a meditation on friendship and mortality, showing the love that Gilgamesh and Enkidu have for one another and the extended journey Gilgamesh undertakes after his friend's death to find the secret of eternal life. Of course, every effort Gilgamesh makes in his attempt to gain immortality is doomed to failure, but at the end of the epic, he returns to his city of Uruk, apparently content that what he has achieved there as king should be his lasting legacy after his death.

Although in both the Akkadian epic and the Sumerian tales Gilgamesh is a semi-divine being and superhuman hero, he is based on an actual human ruler. The historical Gilgamesh ruled the city-state of Uruk sometime between 2800 and 2500 BCE. Legends about the mythologized Gilgamesh begin to appear in Sumerian some four to five hundred years later. The story was then lost for about three thousand years; the modern rediscovery of the tale happened in 1853, when Austen Henry Layard, Hormuzd Rassam, and W. K. Loftus found the tablets in the remains of the Royal Library of Ashurbanipal in the ruins of Nineveh, capital of the Assyrian Empire, which is near modern-day Mosul, Iraq.

Gilgamesh and Enkidu

One of the most famous friendships in all of human storytelling is that between Gilgamesh and Enkidu. At the beginning, Enkidu is a hairy wild man who knows nothing of human customs and who is sent by the gods to moderate Gilgamesh's excesses as king. Enkidu is civilized first by having sexual relations with a prostitute named Shamhat and then by being brought to a shepherd's camp where he is taught how to eat and drink as humans do and where his hair is shaven and shorn and he dons clothing as humans do. Enkidu goes to Uruk intending to challenge Gilgamesh and to put a stop to the king's practice of droit du seigneur, *which Enkidu finds abhorrent, but instead of killing Gilgamesh, he ends up becoming his best friend and companion in arms. Gilgamesh, for his part, is delighted to have finally found a companion who is truly his equal, and from that point on, the two are inseparable.*

Once there was a mighty king named Gilgamesh. His mother was a goddess and his father a great king. Enki himself shaped Gilgamesh's body, gave him his stature and his strength, his beauty of face, his thick wavy hair and beard, and all things that make a man beautiful to behold. No one could best Gilgamesh, either in sport or in battle, and he ruled as king over the city of Uruk as his father Lugalbanda had done before him, and his father's predecessor, the mighty Enmerkar, son of Utu the sun-god, before him.

Gilgamesh was mighty and the king of Uruk, but he did not rule either wisely or well. The young men he summoned to contest after contest, and would not let them go home to their mothers even after he had bested every one. When it came time for the young women to be wed, Gilgamesh took them for himself on their bride-night, only letting them go to their young husbands after he had had them.

The women of Uruk raised their voices to Anu, saying, "O great Anu, O mightiest among the gods, we pray your mercy on our behalf. This Gilgamesh rules us neither wisely nor well. He keeps our sons at his contests day and night, and never does he let them come home even after he has bested every one. And when our daughters are to be wed, he takes them for himself on their bride-night, not giving them to their rightful husbands until after he has had his way with them. O Anu, spare us! Save us from the rapacity of Gilgamesh!"

Anu saw the misdeeds of Gilgamesh, and he heard the cry of the women of Uruk. Anu said, "Let Aruru come forth. Let her create one who is the equal of Gilgamesh. Let him then be sent to Uruk to teach Gilgamesh a lesson!"

And so Aruru heeded the command of Anu. She took a piece of clay and threw it down upon the Earth. From the clay, she made Enkidu, and Ninurta granted to him his own strength. Enkidu had the form of a man, but he was all covered with long hair, and the tresses of his head hung unkempt over his shoulders and down his back. Enkidu knew neither mother nor father; the offspring of silence was he.

Enkidu lived in the wilds among the gazelles, and the gazelles accounted him as one of themselves. Together they ran and grazed and went to the waterhole to drink, and like the gazelles, Enkidu knew nothing of human speech or human customs.

One day, a hunter lay in wait near the watering hole, hoping to catch a gazelle. There he spied Enkidu coming down to the water with his herd. The hunter watched as Enkidu went around the watering hole, pulling up all the traps the hunter had laid to catch his prey. The hunter came back a second day and a third, and each was like the day before: Enkidu came to the watering hole and destroyed all the traps the hunter had laid.

Not knowing what else to do, the hunter went to his father and told him what he had seen. "Every day, this hairy, wild man comes down to the watering hole with the gazelles. He has the strength of a god, and every snare I set he destroys. I am afraid of him, and I do not know what to do."

The hunter's father said, "There is only one thing to do: go to Uruk, and tell King Gilgamesh what you have seen. Gilgamesh is the mightiest in the land; he will know what is to be done, and he will defeat this creature if that is what is needed."

The hunter took his father's advice and set out for Uruk the next morning. He went to the palace where he begged an audience of Gilgamesh. "O Gilgamesh, O mighty King of Uruk, I need your help. A hairy, wild man comes and destroys all the snares I set for game. Truly he has the strength of a god, and I am afraid of him. Please help me, for I have not been able to catch anything to feed my family for many days."

Gilgamesh said, "You must go back to the watering hole, but take the prostitute Shamhat with you. When the wild man appears, have her stand before him and remove her garments. Surely he will be entranced by her beauty and will wish to lie with her. Once he has done that, the herd will no longer account him as one of their own, and he will leave your snares alone."

The hunter did as Gilgamesh said. He went and asked Shamhat the prostitute to go with him, and she agreed, readily. Together the hunter and Shamhat went to the watering hole, and there they lay in wait for Enkidu and his herd. They waited one day, then two days, and on the third day, Enkidu and the gazelles appeared. Enkidu grazed with the herd and played in the water with them and moved about with them as though he were one of them. The hunter said, "There! There is the one I told you about, the hairy, wild man who lives with the gazelles! Go to him, reveal your body, and lie with him. Then maybe the herd will shun him, and I will be able to catch game again."

Then Shamhat came out of hiding and stood on the shore of the watering hole. When she was sure Enkidu was looking at her, she let her shift fall to the ground, revealing her naked body. Enkidu saw the beauty of Shamhat, and he greatly desired her. He went to her, and together they lay on the grass on top of her shift, which she laid out like a fine sheet on a beautiful bed. Enkidu lay in delight with Shamhat. For six days and seven nights they lay together, delighting in one another the whole time. When finally Enkidu's desire was sated, he went to rejoin his herd, but they no longer recognized him. They ran away from him, refusing to let him come near, and when Enkidu tried to run after them, he found that his legs had greatly weakened. He could no longer run among them as he used to do, for Shamhat had taken the wildness from him and replaced it with a man's reason.

So Enkidu went back to where Shamhat sat watching him. Enkidu sat at her feet, and she said to him, "Enkidu, you are as handsome as a god, and as strong. You shouldn't stay here among the beasts; you belong in the cities of men. I will take you back to my city, to Uruk, where Gilgamesh the mighty rules over all, and the temples of Anu and Ishtar rise above the plain in all their splendor."

Enkidu replied, "Yes, take me to your city! I desire to see its temples and to meet this Gilgamesh. There I shall challenge him, and we shall see which of us is mightiest."

"We will go to Uruk, and you shall taste of its delights. There are festivals with music and dancing, where the drummers and flute players play all day long. The prostitutes are so beautiful, none can withstand their charms. But put aside thoughts of challenging Gilgamesh; he is favored of the gods, and no man may best him, in sport or in battle."

In Uruk, Gilgamesh slept in his kingly bed, and he had a dream. It was a strange dream, and he did not know what it meant. So he went to his goddess-mother, the lady Ninsun, to see what she might make of it. "Mother, I have had the strangest dream. I would like to tell it to you to see what you will make of it."

"Tell me your dream, my son," said Ninsun, "and I will apply all my wisdom to it."

"In my dream, a great stone fell from the sky. It fell down into the center of Uruk, and there it sat. All the people gathered around it and wondered at it. I tried to lift the stone, but it was too heavy. I tried to roll the stone away, but I could not move it. And all the while, the people of Uruk gathered around the stone, praising it and kissing it.

"Then something changed. I found that I loved this great stone as a man loves his wife. I loved it as dearly as my own life. And when I loved the stone, I suddenly was able to move it. I picked up the stone and brought it back to you, Mother, where I laid it at your feet, and you said you would turn it into my equal. Tell me, what does this mean?"

"I think I see what this dream portends," said Ninsun. "There is one who is coming who you will love as a man loves his wife, who you will love as dearly as your own life. He will be your equal, and together you will have many adventures. He will save your life, and you will save his."

That night, Gilgamesh went to his rest, and again he had a dream. He dreamed of an axe that fell from the sky, and again all the people of Uruk gathered around it and praised it. Gilgamesh found that he loved the axe as he had loved the stone in the dream before, and just as in that dream, he picked up the axe and brought it to lay at Ninsun's feet.

In the morning, Gilgamesh asked his mother Ninsun what the dream foretold, and she said to him, "My son, this is like the dream of the stone. One is coming who you will love as dearly as your own life, and he will be your equal. He will save your life, and you will save his, and his strength will be like that of a god."

Hearing this, Gilgamesh rejoiced. "May Ellil make it so! I wish to have such a friend and such an equal. May it come true!"

Then it came time for Shamhat to take Enkidu away from the wild places that had been his home. She took her garment and rent it. Part of it she put on herself, and the other part she wrapped around Enkidu. Shamhat took Enkidu to an encampment of shepherds that lived nearby. When the shepherds saw Enkidu, they all gathered around him, wondering. "How like Gilgamesh he is, in stature and in build. This must be Enkidu, of whom we have already heard, for his strength is that of a god."

The shepherds invited Enkidu in and treated him as an honored guest. They set before him bread and good beer, but Enkidu had never seen these before and did not know what to do with them. Shamhat said to him, "Eat the bread, Enkidu! You need good food to keep you strong. Drink the beer! It is one of the delights of life."

And so Enkidu ate his fill and drank of the beer, seven whole goblets full. Soon he was feeling very merry and sang songs. When the meal was done, the barbers of the camp came to Enkidu. They shaved him and anointed him with oil. They shaved away all the beast from him; they cut his locks and trimmed his beard and dressed him in warrior's garments, and thus it was that Enkidu became a man. Then Enkidu lived among the shepherds, chasing away wolves and lions, watching over the people and their flocks. And when Enkidu slept, he did so with Shamhat the prostitute, and they continued to delight in one another every night.

One night as Enkidu and Shamhat lay together, Enkidu happened to look up and saw a man standing not far away. He seemed to wish to speak to Enkidu, so Enkidu said to Shamhat, "Do you know that man? Do you know what he wants? Bring him here so that I may find out what he needs of me."

Shamhat brought him over, and Enkidu said, "Tell me, what is it you want? How may I aid you?"

The man said, "I was invited to a wedding banquet in Uruk. That is a time when a man takes a wife, and everyone celebrates. But in Uruk, the king demands that the young woman not spend her bride-night with her husband. Instead, Gilgamesh takes the woman back to his palace and has his way with her. Gilgamesh says that this is his right because he is king." And as the man spoke, his voice shook with anger.

Enkidu heard what the man said, and he became angry as well. He set out for Uruk that instant, and Shamhat went with him. When Enkidu entered the city, all the people looked at him in wonder. "Who can this be? He is just as tall as Gilgamesh and just as well made in his body. Surely this man has the strength of a god!"

Enkidu went to the place where the marriage feast was being held. He saw the marriage-house all arranged with a fine bed, a place to be blessed by the goddess of weddings. Then Enkidu saw Gilgamesh, a man like him in stature and build. Gilgamesh took the hand of a young woman dressed in fine linen and golden jewelry, and led her to the marriage-house. He ushered the young woman in, but before Gilgamesh could enter himself, Enkidu stood in the way and put his foot in the door. Gilgamesh was enraged at this presumption. He grappled with Enkidu, and combat was joined.

Up and down the town square they fought. They landed such blows that the doors shuddered in their jambs. They knocked one another down with such force that all the windows shuddered in their frames. Up and down the town square they fought, neither one able to get the best of the other. They fought as the day went from morning to afternoon and then as afternoon wore away to sunset, but neither one could claim himself the victor. Finally, they stood panting and glaring at one another, and Gilgamesh said, "You have done a thing that no other in the land has ever been able to do. You have fought with me up and down the town square, landing blows and knocking me down, and I have done the same to you, and yet neither of us is the victor. None before you has done this feat. Come, let us clasp hands and kiss one another, for I think we should be friends!"

Gilgamesh and the Bull of Heaven

In the story that precedes this one, Gilgamesh and Enkidu have gone to the Mountains of Cedar to slay the forest giant Humbaba. With that task accomplished, Gilgamesh and Enkidu arrive home safely only to find that another threat awaits them. The goddess Ishtar sees how beautiful and brave Gilgamesh is and proposes marriage to him, but when he refuses, she sends the Bull of Heaven down to destroy him. Of course, Gilgamesh and Enkidu manage to slay the Bull, but the combination of this deed and the slaying of Humbaba will prove fatal to Enkidu. The episode of the Bull of Heaven ends with Gilgamesh and Enkidu being welcomed to a banquet in their honor, but in the following story, we learn that the gods have looked unfavorably on Gilgamesh's exploits and declare that one of the two friends must die.

The story of the Bull of Heaven is one of those having a parallel in the Sumerian version of the epic. The basic plot of both versions is the same. Gilgamesh comes home from killing Humbaba (Sumerian Huwawa), and Ishtar (Sumerian Inanna) proposes marriage. Gilgamesh refuses, and so Ishtar/Inanna, in a fit of temper, sends the Bull to destroy Gilgamesh and his city. In the Sumerian version, Gilgamesh attempts to placate Inanna by offering her treasure and animals from his flocks, while in the Akkadian version, Ishtar tries to get Gilgamesh to agree to her proposal by promising to enrich him and increase his political power. Gilgamesh's refusal in the Akkadian version also is much more forceful: he recites a litany of the fates of Ishtar's past lovers and states baldly that he refuses to become yet another male to first become her lover and then have the bad luck to fall afoul of her.

Gilgamesh came home to Uruk. He came home from his quest and found that his clothing, body, armor, and weapons were dusty and spattered with blood. Gilgamesh took off his dirty clothing, and he cleaned his armor and weapons. Then Gilgamesh cleaned himself well in the bath, washing all of the dirt of his adventure from his body and his hair and beard. He put on fresh, clean clothing. He combed out his hair and put on his crown.

Then the lady Ishtar saw Gilgamesh. She saw how well dressed he was, how well made he was in his body and how fair of face, and she desired him greatly. Ishtar went to Gilgamesh and said, "O Gilgamesh, come to me and be my bridegroom! Let us delight in one another, as husband and wife! Marry me, and I will give you riches beyond compare, a chariot made of gold and lapis lazuli, with lions to pull it for you. I will give you a house made with fragrant cedar, and when you arrive home, even the threshold and your throne shall kiss your feet. Kings and lords from all the lands around will honor you and bring you tribute. All your flocks will increase two- and three-fold, and your beasts of burden will never tire. Come to me! Marry me! Let us be husband and wife together!"

Gilgamesh replied, "Lady Ishtar, were you to give me all that and nothing else, still I would be in your debt. Never could I match those rich gifts. What happens to me when you no longer delight in my company, when you no longer wish to share my bed, when my body no longer sets yours aflame with desire?

"My lady, well I know what happens to those who accept your offers. Well I know what happens to lovers who give in to your charms. How many of those have there been now? How many have you loved and discarded? Perhaps we should count them together. There was Tammuz, who loved you first, but who now sits in the Underworld where he weeps in perpetuity. Next came the *allallu-*bird, but when he displeased you, you broke his wing, and now he sits in the forest crying for pain. After that, you loved the lion, and when you were through with him, you dug for him a pit, and when he fell in, you left him there. You loved the horse, but in return for his devotion, you gave him a whip and spurs to make him gallop endless miles, and for his reward at the end a pail of muddy water.

"Once you loved a shepherd. He toiled for you, baking fresh bread, slaughtering and cooking a lamb for you, every day. And his reward? To be turned into a wolf, driven away by his friends, chased down and bitten by the dogs. And after him was Ishullanu, the gardener. Every day, he brought you a basket full of dates. Him you looked upon with desire, saying, 'Come to my bed! Touch me in my private parts! Let me caress you, let us delight in one another,' but he refused you again and again, and only gave in because you would not relent. And when he pleased you no longer, you turned him into a frog, and now he sits lamenting in the middle of his withered garden, for he no longer is able to labor in it as he used to.

"Come, my lady," said Gilgamesh, "Why should I accept your offer, generous as it is, knowing what has happened to everyone who has loved you before? I doubt that even I would be able to escape such a fate, should I displease you."

Hearing Gilgamesh's words, Ishtar flew into a rage. She ran shrieking into heaven and went to her father Anu and mother Antu, tears streaming down her cheeks. "Mother! Father! Come to my aid! Gilgamesh has been saying terrible things about me! He heaps insult after insult upon me, and it is unbearable."

Anu said, "What did you say to him? Did you provoke him so that he spoke to you thus?"

Ishtar replied, "Father, give me the Bull of Heaven. Give it to me, and I shall send it to slay Gilgamesh and trample his palace into dust. And if you will not give me the Bull, then I shall destroy the Underworld. The dead I shall raise and set them upon the living to devour them until there are more dead than living upon the Earth."

"If I give you the Bull of Heaven," said Anu, "then famine shall descend upon Uruk, famine lasting seven years. What provision have you made for the people and their beasts? Have you set aside grain and chaff and hay for them?"

"Yes, I have grain and chaff and hay aplenty, enough for seven years," said Ishtar.

And so Anu gave to Ishtar the Bull of Heaven. Ishtar led the Bull down onto the Earth, and together they journeyed until they reached Uruk. When the Bull entered Uruk, the trees and the plants all withered and died. The waters of the Euphrates diminished, receding by seven full cubits. The Bull uttered a great snort, and a pit opened beneath the feet of the men of Uruk. A hundred men toppled into the pit. The Bull uttered a second snort, and another pit claimed two hundred men of Uruk. At its third snort, a pit opened at the feet of Enkidu, who fell in up to his waist.

Enkidu jumped out of the pit and grabbed the Bull by its horns. Enraged, the Bull spat in Enkidu's face. It lifted its tail and poured dung all over him.

Enkidu called to Gilgamesh for aid. "Come, my friend! We must defend our city and our people! I have tried myself against the Bull of Heaven, and I know its strength and what it can do, and I know how we might defeat it. I will grab hold of the beast's tail and brace my foot against the back of its leg. Then you must take your knife and slay it as butchers do cattle. Slide your knife into its neck behind the skull, and do it quickly while I hold its tail!"

Enkidu went behind the Bull and grabbed hold of its tail. He braced his foot against the back of its leg. Then Gilgamesh drew his knife and plunged it with skill and strength into the spot on its neck behind the skull, and the Bull fell down, dead. The two friends opened up the Bull's chest and pulled out its heart. They went to the temple and offered the heart to Shamash, bowing down before him. Then they went and sat together, side by side, like brothers.

When Ishtar saw that the Bull had been slain and its heart offered to Shamash, she shrieked in fury and climbed upon the walls of Uruk. "Woe to you, Gilgamesh! Woe to you for your insults and for killing the Bull of Heaven!"

Enkidu heard the shrieks of Ishtar. He pulled off one of the Bull's haunches and flung it toward her. "Here is your portion," he cried, "and if I could catch you, I would do the same to you, and wrap your arms in the guts of the Bull besides!"

Ishtar sent a summons throughout the city. She called together all the courtesans and prostitutes, and set them to mourning over the haunch of the Bull. Gilgamesh, meanwhile, called together the craftsmen of the city. They sawed off the Bull's horns, each weighing thirty *minas* of lapis lazuli. So great were they that they could hold six *kor* of oil.

Gilgamesh took the horns, hallowed them for the anointing of the god Lugalbanda, and filled them with holy oil, and when that was done, Gilgamesh hung the horns in his bedchamber. Then Enkidu and Gilgamesh went to the river to wash the sweat and dust and blood of battle from their bodies and clothing, and when they were refreshed, they returned to the palace in a chariot, where they stood hand in hand.

As they drove through the streets, the people of Uruk gathered to shout their praises. Gilgamesh asked the serving girls of his household, "Tell me, who is the most beautiful of all men, and who the bravest of all heroes?" And they replied, "Why, Gilgamesh is the most beautiful of all men and Enkidu the bravest of all heroes!"

Then Gilgamesh and Enkidu went into the palace where a great feast had been laid in their honor, and there they ate and drank and made merry long into the night.

The Wanderings of Gilgamesh

After killing the Bull of Heaven, Enkidu is cursed by the gods for his presumption. Enkidu falls ill, and after many days of suffering, he dies. Gilgamesh is heartbroken at the loss of his companion, and he becomes more aware than ever of death and of his own mortality. He wanders in the wilderness, looking for Utnapishtim, the man who survived the Great Flood, thinking to get from him the secret of eternal life. In the process, Gilgamesh becomes a wild man of a sort himself, living in the open, wearing animal skins for clothing, and hunting prey for his food. It is not until Gilgamesh encounters Utnapishtim and hears his story that Gilgamesh is restored to a more civilized state.

Having sung a lament for Enkidu and buried him with all ceremony as is fit and proper, Gilgamesh sat and wept. He wept not only for his dead friend but also for himself. "Enkidu, best of companions, is dead. He has gone into the Underworld. Never more will he see the light of the sun or taste of clear water or freshly baked bread. Never more will he be at my side through thick and thin, my strong, brave companion Enkidu. For he has died and gone down into the Underworld, as we all must go. Even I, Gilgamesh, King of Uruk, child of the gods, must one day die.

"I do not wish to die. Death is a fearsome thing. I am afraid of dying. I must find a way to cheat death, to escape that fate. I will go into the wild and look for Utnapishtim, for he of all human beings was made immortal by the gods. I shall find him and ask him how I might go about cheating death myself."

And so Gilgamesh went into the wilderness. When fierce beasts attacked him, Gilgamesh fought with them. He killed the beasts, skinned them, and roasted their flesh and ate it. Gilgamesh wandered long in the wilderness, clad in the pelts of lions and hyenas and gazelles, living on what game he could catch, always looking for the way to the abode of Utnapishtim.

Shamash, the sun-god, looked down upon Gilgamesh and grew worried. "Gilgamesh, what is this that you do to yourself? Why do you wander the wilderness, clad in the pelts of animals, ever wandering and never resting? You will never seek what you find."

Gilgamesh replied, "Why should I rest now? When I am dead, I shall rest forever. Why should I stop wandering now? At least now I can still see the light of the sun; in the Underworld, all is darkness and dust, forever. No, I will not stop. I will wander as I may; it is my will."

And so Gilgamesh continued to wander the world until he came to the towering mountain of Mashu, who crest meets the sky and whose roots went down into the bottom of the Underworld itself. Gilgamesh reached the gates to the mountain and found them guarded by two scorpion-beings, fearsome to behold and deadly. They shone with a radiance nearly as bright as Shamash himself, for it was their duty to guard him as he rose in the morning and set in the evening. Gilgamesh looked upon the scorpion-beings and fell to his knees. He covered his face in fear before them.

"Who is this who comes before us?" said one scorpion-being to the other. "Why is he here?"

The other replied, "I know who this is. This is Gilgamesh, King of Uruk, and the blood of the gods flows in his veins." Then the second scorpion-being looked upon Gilgamesh and said "You there, who kneels before us, why have you come to our mountain? What is it you seek here? Explain yourself!"

"I am looking for the abode of Utnapishtim," said Gilgamesh. "I have wandered the whole world looking for the way to his abode, for he has the secret of eternal life, and I wish to learn that of him for myself."

The first scorpion-being said, "Very well, we will tell you the way, for never has a mortal man ever found his way to our mountain gate. But be warned: the way you go is dark and lightless, for it is the path Shamash himself follows after he sets in the west at nightfall. Have you the courage to brave that darkness?"

"I have known nothing but darkness and grief since the death of my companion," said Gilgamesh. "What can this new darkness possibly add to that? Tell me the way."

"Very well," said the second scorpion-being. "You must go through these gates and down into the dark tunnel that lies beyond. On, on, on you must go in the darkness, and you must never stop until you reach the other side. Do not stop, no matter how fearful you are! Go on until you see the light of day again. Twelve hours is the journey on the path Shamash follows. Twelve hours must you also journey on, in total darkness."

Then the scorpion-beings opened wide the gates of their mountain, and Gilgamesh walked through them into the darkness that lay beyond. For one hour, Gilgamesh walked. The darkness around him was complete; he could see neither in front of him nor behind. For two hours, Gilgamesh walked, and three and four, and never a ray of light did he see. On and on, Gilgamesh walked, and as he walked, he could feel the great weight of the darkness pressing down upon him. A fifth hour, and a sixth, and a seventh he walked through the darkness, and never a ray of light did he see. An eighth hour he walked on, and he began to think that maybe he had entered the Underworld itself, that he was dead already and would never see the light of day again. But he summoned all his courage and walked on.

At the ninth hour, Gilgamesh found hope, for a cool breeze blew along the path. His strength renewed, Gilgamesh walked on for a tenth hour, and an eleventh, and at the end of the twelfth hour, he could see a glimmer of light ahead of him, the light of the morning sun. Gilgamesh rejoiced and ran toward the light. He ran out into this bright new place and found himself in the orchard of the gods, where fresh grapes grew on vines of cornelian, where trees of lapis lazuli bore fruit of their own that perfumed the entire orchard, and all sparkled in the light of the morning sun.

Gilgamesh walked through the orchard, looking about him in delight. When he came to the other side, there he found a tavern, which had been built on the shore of the sea. The owner of the tavern was a wise old woman named Siduri. She saw Gilgamesh approaching and knew him for one who had the blood of the gods in his veins. But he was clad all in the pelts of animals and had a fearsome, wild aspect, and so Siduri barred the door of the tavern so that Gilgamesh could not enter. Then Siduri went up onto the roof, the better to watch what Gilgamesh might do.

Gilgamesh saw the old woman bar the door of the tavern, and a few moments later, he saw her up on the roof, watching him. "Old woman," shouted Gilgamesh, "why do you bar your door to me? What have I done that you should fear me? Know this: if you do not open to me willingly, I shall break down your door myself!"

"I barred the door because I do not know who you are or why you are here," said Siduri. "Tell me of yourself, that I may judge whether it is wise to open to you."

"I am Gilgamesh, King of Uruk. My brave companion Enkidu and I slew the forest giant Humbaba. Together we slew the Bull of Heaven. Together we hunted lions in the mountains, and there we slew many."

"A likely story," said Siduri. "If you really are a king and a hero like you say, why is your face so gaunt and your hair so matted? Why do you go about dressed in dirty beast pelts? You certainly look nothing whatever like a king and certainly nothing like Gilgamesh, of whom I have heard."

"My face is gaunt and my hair is matted and I wear beast pelts because I have been wandering in the wilderness. I wander the wilderness because my brave companion Enkidu, who bore many dangers with me and who I loved most dearly, has died. He was cursed by the gods and has gone down into the Underworld to drink dust. After my friend died, I became afraid of death, and now I am seeking the abode of Utnapishtim, that I may ask of him the secret to eternal life.

"Can you tell me the way, O innkeeper? How may I find the abode of Utnapishtim? If I must cross the sea, I will do it. If I must cross the desert, I will do it. If I must climb a mountain, I will do it. Tell me the way, if you know it. And if you do not know it, I shall wander the wilderness until I find it for myself."

"This is a fool's errand you are on," replied Siduri. "No one has ever crossed that sea but Shamash himself. And even if you could make the crossing, it is so dangerous that you would never survive it. Even if you sail the sea, the Waters of Death are halfway between here and there and block the way forward. You cannot get to Utnapishtim without crossing them. What will you do then?

"But if cross you must, you must go to Urshanabi, the boatman of Utnapishtim. You will find him over yonder, with the stone-beings who are his companions and shipmates. You will find them in the pine forest, cutting down saplings to use for barge poles. Go to Urshanabi, and ask whether he will take you across. But if he will not take you, there will be no way across for you, and you must go back the way you came!"

Gilgamesh went into the pine forest where he saw Urshanabi at work with the stone-beings. Gilgamesh drew his axe and his dagger and then fell upon them. Urshanabi saw Gilgamesh coming and took up his own axe to defend himself and his companions, but he was no match for Gilgamesh. Gilgamesh knocked Urshanabi down, and he lay stunned on the ground. Then Gilgamesh attacked the stone-beings, shattering their bodies and throwing the pieces into the river that flowed through the forest.

When the stone-beings had all been slain, Gilgamesh went back to Urshanabi and stood over him. Urshanabi opened his eyes and saw Gilgamesh standing there. Gilgamesh said, "Tell me your name."

"I am Urshanabi, boatman to Utnapishtim. Who are you?"

"I am Gilgamesh, King of Uruk. My brave companion Enkidu and I slew the forest giant Humbaba. Together we slew the Bull of

Heaven. Together we hunted lions in the mountains, and there we slew many. I took the path of Shamash under the mountains, and I am seeking the abode of Utnapishtim."

"A likely story," said Urshanabi. "If you really are a king and a hero like you say, why is your face so gaunt and your hair so matted? Why do you go about dressed in dirty beast pelts? You certainly look nothing whatever like a king and certainly nothing like Gilgamesh, of whom I have heard."

"My face is gaunt and my hair is matted and I wear beast pelts because I have been wandering in the wilderness. I wander the wilderness because my brave companion Enkidu, who bore many dangers with me and who I loved most dearly, has died. He was cursed by the gods and has gone down into the Underworld to drink dust. After my friend died, I became afraid of death, and now I am seeking the abode of Utnapishtim, that I may ask of him the secret to eternal life. Now, tell me how I may get there, for the innkeeper said that you know the way."

"I do know the way," said Urshanabi, "but you have taken from us the means to get there. I cannot manage the boat without the help of the stone-beings, nor without the barge poles they were making, and you have killed them all."

"Tell me what you need," said Gilgamesh, "and I will provide it."

"Cut down pine saplings, and strip them to use as barge poles. We will need 120. When the saplings are stripped, put a boss on the end of each of them."

Gilgamesh took his axe and cut down 120 saplings. Then he took his dagger and stripped them. When that was done, he put a boss on the end of each of them. Then Gilgamesh helped Urshanabi launch the boat into the sea. Together Gilgamesh and Urshanabi rowed the boat. Now, the journey from the shore to the Waters of Death normally would take two months, but with Gilgamesh's help, they arrived in only three days.

At the edge of the Waters of Death, Urshanabi said, "Take up a barge pole, Gilgamesh, and punt us across the waters. But take care not to touch the waters, for they will shrivel up your hand!"

Gilgamesh took up the first pole and began to punt them across the Waters of Death while Urshanabi steered. Soon the first barge pole was no longer of any use, so Gilgamesh took up the second. And when the second was no longer of any use, Gilgamesh took up the third, and the fourth, and the fifth. After he had punted them a long way but before they had arrived at the other side, Gilgamesh had used up all the poles.

"What will we do now?" said Urshanabi. "We have no more poles."

"Strip off your garments," said Gilgamesh. "I shall strip mine also, and we shall use them for a sail."

"But there is neither mast nor yardarm on this craft," said Urshanabi.

"I shall be both mast and yardarm," said Gilgamesh. And so Gilgamesh and Urshanabi stripped off their garments, and Gilgamesh stood up in the middle of the boat and held his arms open wide. Urshanabi took the garments and made of them a sail, hanging it from Gilgamesh's mighty arms while his body served for a mast, and in this way they sailed across to the place where Utnapishtim made his abode.

Now, Utnapishtim happened to look out over the water as Urshanabi and Gilgamesh were sailing toward him. Utnapishtim said to himself, "I see there Urshanabi, my boatman, but who is that with him? I do not recognize him at all."

Soon enough, Urshanabi and Gilgamesh arrived on the shore where they found Utnapishtim waiting for them.

"My boatman I know," said Untapishtim to Gilgamesh, "but who are you?"

"I am Gilgamesh, King of Uruk. My brave companion Enkidu and I slew the forest giant Humbaba. Together we slew the Bull of

Heaven. Together we hunted lions in the mountains, and there we slew many. I took the path of Shamash under the mountains, and I sailed across the sea and across the Waters of Death, for I am seeking Utnapishtim."

"Utnapishtim you have found, for he stands here before you. But I do not believe your tale of yourself. If you really are a king and a hero like you say, why is your face so gaunt and your hair so matted? Why do you go about dressed in dirty beast pelts? You certainly look nothing whatever like a king and certainly nothing like Gilgamesh, of whom I have heard."

"My face is gaunt and my hair is matted and I wear beast pelts because I have been wandering in the wilderness. I wander the wilderness because my brave companion Enkidu, who bore many dangers with me and who I loved most dearly, has died. He was cursed by the gods and has gone down into the Underworld to drink dust. After my friend died, I became afraid of death, and that is why I have sought you out, that I may ask you the secret of eternal life."

"Oh, Gilgamesh," said Utnapishtim, "the blood of the gods runs in your veins, and yet you behave thus? You were given a throne and riches, and you have cast them all away in exchange for a life of endless toil in the wilderness and a fool's errand. Death comes for everyone in the end, and no one ever sees his face. Death creeps up on them and takes them unawares. We may build fine houses and bridges and boats, but nowhere may we hide from Death. Those he takes are gone forever, and we never see them again. This is the fate the Annunaki have decreed. Life they have given, but also death, and the gods may not be gainsaid."

Gilgamesh and Utnapishtim

This final chapter of the Epic of Gilgamesh *contains a retelling of the Sumerian flood myth by Utnapishtim, the builder of the ark and the only man ever to attain immortality. When Utnapishtim is done with his tale, Gilgamesh asks him how he might become immortal as well. Utnapishtim tells him that he must stay awake for six days and seven nights, whereupon the exhausted Gilgamesh promptly lies down and sleeps for that much time. Despairing of ever reaching his goal, Gilgamesh prepares to leave Utnapishtim, but the latter's wife reminds him that there is one other possible route for Gilgamesh to take: go to the bottom of the sea and find the plant of life. Gilgamesh succeeds in this, only to lose the plant to a thieving serpent when he is making the journey home to his own city.*

Gilgamesh and his companion Urshanabi travel together until they reach Uruk. Upon their arrival, Gilgamesh boasts to Urshanabi of the prosperity of Uruk and proposes a tour of the city walls. The epic ends here, with Gilgamesh safely returned home and proud of his accomplishments as the King of Uruk.

Gilgamesh stood on the shore and looked at Utnapishtim. Then he said, "At first I thought that you might be like a god and that I would need to fight you. But now that I see you, I understand that you are a man, just like me. Tell me, O eldest one, how is it that you came to be immortal? How might this gift be obtained? For I do not wish to die. I do not wish to go into the Underworld to drink dust."

"I will tell you this," said Utnapishtim, "even though it is a secret known only to the gods. Once I lived in the city of Shuruppak, a fine city on the banks of the Euphrates wherein even the gods dwelt once. The great god Anu had become angry with the people, and he resolved to send down a Great Flood to wash them all away. He took counsel of Ellil and Ninurta, and they agreed that this was a good plan. Even Ea, the most wise, took an oath that this thing should be done. But when Ea did so, he went near my house and whispered into the walls his oath to bring the Great Flood, and so I learned what it was the gods resolved to do.

"Ea also whispered to me that I should build a great boat and place therein every kind of living thing. He whispered to me how long the boat should be and how wide, and he told me to put a roof over it. I said to Ea, 'O mighty Ea, wisest of the wise, I hear your command,

and I obey. But surely the elders of my city will notice the boat as I build it. What shall I say to them when they ask me what it is I do?'

"Ea said to me, 'Tell them that you have run afoul of Ellil and so can no longer live in the city. Tell them that I have given you the command to build the boat, that I am going to take you to live with me in my dwelling in the Apsu. Tell them that if they help you build the boat, I will shower upon them fresh bread and fresh fish, enough for a feast!'

"And so it was that I commenced building the boat. I hired workmen to fell the trees and mill the lumber, to construct the hull and put inside it the decks. After five days, the hull was complete. The boat measured ten rods high, and it covered a full acre of land. Six decks it had, and the inside was divided into nine compartments. Every day, I slaughtered lambs and oxen to feed my workers. I fed them well; every day was like a feast!

"When all was finished, I loaded the boat with all my goods and with food and water for people and beasts alike. I took aboard all of my family and also workmen who were skilled in their crafts. I took aboard the animals, as Ea had instructed me, wild beasts and tame alike. I took all these things aboard and waited for the sign Ea said would come, the shower of fresh bread and fresh fish, enough for a feast!

"Soon enough that sign came, and so I looked to the heavens to see what would happen next. I watched the sun rise, and as Shamash started his path across the sky, a great wall of black clouds rose up behind him, and within those clouds stormed Adad, the god of rain, and his attendants stormed along with him. The Annunaki came, too, and wherever they passed, they called down lightning that struck down trees and destroyed houses and breached the city walls. The river rose and began to overflow its banks, and still the storm wind of Adad continued to blow, and the rain came down.

"Then the whole world went black as night, and for a moment, it was still. And then came the Great Flood, a great surge of water that swept away all before it. It scoured the land clean of all living things and rose many rods above the tops of the highest trees. The water climbed up the sides of the mountains, covering all but the peaks of the very tallest.

"The gods looked down upon the flood they had unleashed, and they became frightened. They ran away to their abode in the heavens where they sat cowering like dogs. When the goddess Belet-ili saw what the gods had wrought, she wailed and lamented. 'Woe that I agreed to this course! Woe that I had a part in the destruction the flood has wrought! For all my children have been swept away, and now they float in the water like fish.'

"The Annunaki looked down at what they had wrought, and they quailed there in their abode in the heavens. They looked down on what they had wrought, and they wept for sorrow and for shame. But on and on the storm raged, for this is what the Annunaki had commanded. For six days and seven nights did it rain, for six days and seven nights did the winds blow a gale. And on the seventh day, the rain stopped, and the winds quieted, and the waves of the ocean that had been like very hills quieted, and my boat floated upon a calm sea under the light of Shamash.

"I opened one of the portholes in the side of the boat and saw the light of Shamash. I looked out, and everywhere I looked was nothing but sea, except for fourteen islands that had been the highest mountain peaks. I saw what had become of the world, and I wept bitter tears. We floated upon the waters for a while, but then the boat ran aground on Mount Nimush, and there we sat for six days. On the seventh day, I released a dove, to see what had become of the land, but the dove returned, for there was no place for her to perch. I did the same with a swallow, and it, too, came back. Then I brought out a raven and let it go, but it did not come back, for the waters had begun to recede, and it was able to find food.

"When the raven did not return, I sacrificed to the gods. I burned incense there on the top of the mountain, and the scent of it rose into the nostrils of the gods and pleased them. As the incense burned and the smoke of it arose, the goddess Belet-ili appeared and said, 'Surely this incense will draw all the gods nigh. But let Ellil stay away, for it was his counsel that the world should be destroyed by a Great Flood.'

"Just then, Ellil arrived. He saw the boat and the people and the animals who had survived the flood, and he was most wroth. 'How is it that these have survived? Who is it that told them to prepare, that they might be spared? Who is it that went against the will of the Annunaki?'

"Ninurta said, 'Who else would do such a thing but Ea? Ask him.'

Ea turned to Ellil and said, 'Yes, I did this thing. I saved them. For you did wrong by destroying the whole world. Why punish those who were not guilty? You could have sent lions to eat the ones who did wrong. You could have sent a famine or a plague and still achieved your goal. I did not tell this man our secret but rather sent him a vision of what was to come, and he did as he was commanded. But now you must decide his fate.'

"Ellil went into my boat. He stretched out his hand to me and to my wife and brought us aboard. He bid us kneel before him, then he touched our foreheads and said, 'You were born mortals, but from now on, you shall be immortal. Together you shall dwell in a far land, at the source of all rivers.'

"But the gods are not here. They will not gather together here for you. Perhaps if you go six days and seven nights without sleep, you will find what you seek."

Gilgamesh then sat down, to attempt what Utnapishtim said he must do, but no sooner had his body touched the ground than he was overcome with a deep sleep, and there he lay upon the ground. Utnapishtim said to his wife, "Look! He wanted to become immortal by staying awake, and the moment he touches the ground, he falls asleep!"

His wife said, "Wake him then, and send him back to his own country. Send him home, back the way he came!"

"No, I'll not do that," said Utnapishtim, "for men can be deceitful. Instead, you shall bake for him his daily bread, and each day he sleeps, place one loaf by his head. Then mark on this wall the number of days he has slumbered away. When he awakes, he will see how long he has slept."

Utnapishtim's wife did as her husband commanded her. Each day, she baked a loaf of bread and put it next to Gilgamesh's head where he slept there on the shore, and she marked the number of the days he slept on the nearby wall. One day Gilgamesh slept, then two, then three and four, then five, then six. And each loaf of bread began to harden and then molder as time went by. Finally, on the dawn of the seventh day, Utnapishtim shook Gilgamesh by the shoulder and said, "Gilgamesh, awaken!"

Gilgamesh sat up and said, "What is this? No sooner did I lay down to sleep but you awaken me!"

Utnapishtim pointed to the loaves of bread and said, "You have slept for six days and seven nights. Look here at these loaves of bread. My wife baked one for every day you slept, and you can see that they have all begun to harden and molder. Also, we marked the days of your slumber on this wall. You will see there are seven markings."

Gilgamesh sorrowed at this, saying, "Alas, for no matter where I go, Death is always there, snapping at my heels! Will I never be free of him?"

Utnapishtim then turned to Urshanabi, the boatman, and said, "Never more shall you come here. You and the man you brought are both banished from this place forever. But these tasks must you do before you bring him home. Draw a hot bath for Gilgamesh, and let him soak in it until all the dust and grime of his weary travels have been washed away. Wash his unkempt hair, and comb it out neatly. Take the beast pelts and cast them into the sea for the tide to take them where it will. And when Gilgamesh is clean and refreshed, give him clothing to wear, garments befitting his station. Restore his body to its natural beauty, so that he may go home to his people without shame."

Urshanabi did as he was commanded. He drew a bath for Gilgamesh and washed and combed his hair. He took the beast pelts and threw them into the sea. And when Gilgamesh was clean and refreshed, Urshanabi dressed him in clean garments befitting his station. Then Gilgamesh and Urshanabi boarded their boat and pushed it out into the surf.

Utnapishtim and his wife stood on the shore watching them go. Suddenly, Utnapishtim's wife said, "Wait! Call them back, for Gilgamesh leaves us without a gift befitting such a guest, a royal guest who has come here after long toil and danger."

Utnapishtim called them back, and when they had beached the boat once more, he said to Gilgamesh, "Before you go, one last secret will I impart to you. In the ocean that flows beneath the earth, there is a plant that will restore an old person's vigor, the Plant of Life. If you go down to that ocean, you will see it growing there. The plant has many thorns; have care when you pluck it! Bring it back with you, and you will have your desire."

Gilgamesh dug a great pit that opened above the ocean that flows beneath the earth. He tied great stones to his feet so that he could descend to the sea floor, then he jumped into the pit and descended to the bottom of the ocean. There he saw the thorny plant, just as Utnapishtim said. Gilgamesh grasped it, and the thorns cut his palm, but he did not pay that any mind. He cut the bonds that held the stones to his feet and rose to the surface. When he broke through into the good, clean air, he shouted, "I have found it! Now I shall be able to cheat death! But first I will test this on some old man of my city to see whether it works, and if it does, I shall take some myself!"

Urshanabi helped Gilgamesh out of the pit, and together they took ship to take Gilgamesh home to his city of Uruk. They crossed the ocean in safety, but a journey of many miles still lay before them. Together they walked in companionship, until one day they stopped by a clear pool that was surrounded by trees. The day was hot and dry, and Gilgamesh wished to refresh himself. He stripped off his clothing and lay it at the edge of the pool, along with the Plant of Life. But while Gilgamesh splashed in the water refreshing himself, a serpent passed nearby. The serpent smelled the scent of the plant and was drawn to it, so it went to the edge of the pool and carried the plant away.

When Gilgamesh came out of the pool, he saw that the plant was gone, but that the serpent had shed its skin after taking it and slithering away. Gilgamesh sat on the ground and wept. "O, all I have endured has been for naught! All the journey, and all the hardship, and all the danger, wasted! I will never again be able to find that plant, and Death shall come for me in time, as he does for everyone."

Gilgamesh and Urshanabi traveled on, stopping only to eat and sleep. And on the next day, they arrived at the city of Uruk. "There is my city, Urshanabi! Is she not glorious? Look at her strong walls, her finely crafted gates! Come, walk with me upon the walls, and you shall see how well my city is built, and how prosperous she is. You shall see the date groves and the Temple of Ishtar and many other things besides, in this, my city. Come!"

Glossary

Adad	God of weather and rain
Adapa	A wise man favored by the gods; unknowingly refuses the gift of immortality
Annunaki	The greater gods
Annunitum	A warrior goddess originally connected with **Ishtar**
Anshar	Mesopotamian god; father of **Anu**; consort of **Kishar**
Anu	Chief god of the Mesopotamian pantheon; one of the **Annunaki**
Anzu Bird	Mythical creature with the head of a lion and the body of a bird; associated with thunder
Apsu (i)	In the Babylonian creation myth, a creator god associated with sweet water

Apsu (ii)	Dwelling-place of **Enki** underground; place of underground sweet water
Aruru	Mesopotamian mother goddess; one of the **Annunaki**
Asushunamir	Eunuch created to help rescue **Ishtar** from the Underworld
Atrahasis	Survivor of the Great Flood and builder of the ark
Aw-ila	God who gives his life to create humans
Babylon	Mesopotamian city; became the seat of the Babylonian Empire and one of the most important ancient urban centers
Belet-ili	A mother goddess; mother of the hero-god **Ninurta**; one of the **Annunaki**
Belili	Sumerian deity; sister of Dumuzi (Akkadian **Tammuz**); also known as Geshtinanna
Bull of Heaven	Possibly a reference to the constellation Taurus; monstrous bull sent by **Ishtar** to kill **Gilgamesh**
Dagan	A god of fertility and agriculture
Damkina	A mother goddess; wife of **Enki**; one of the **Annunaki**
Duranki	A house of the gods
E-kur	Another name for **Duranki**

Ea	God of wisdom, creation, and mischief; often syncretic with **Enki** in Sumerian myths; one of the **Annunaki**
E-galgina	A palace within the Underworld
Ellil	God associated with winds; one of the **Annunaki**
Enki	God of wisdom, creation, and mischief; often syncretic with **Ea** in Akkadian myths; husband of **Damkina**; one of the **Annunaki**
Enkidu	A hairy, wild man sent to tame **Gilgamesh**; becomes Gilgamesh's best friend and companion in arms
Ennugi	Servant to **Ellil**; also associated with canals
Ereshkigal	Goddess of the Underworld; consort of **Nergal**
Eridu	Ancient Sumerian city; considered to be the home of **Enki**
Erra	Warrior god; also associated with the power of the sun; syncretic with **Nergal**
E-sara	House for the gods created by **Marduk**
Etana	Ancient king of **Kish**
Gilgamesh	King of Uruk and protagonist of the *Epic of Gilgamesh*

Gizzida	Sumerian Underworld deity; husband of **Belili**; also known as Ningishzida
Humbaba	A forest giant slain by **Gilgamesh** and **Enkidu**
Igigi	The lesser gods
Ilabrat	Attendant of **Anu**
Ishtar	Goddess of procreation and war; one of the **Annunaki**
Ishullanu	Man who refused to make love to **Ishtar**; mentioned in the *Epic of Gilgamesh*
Kalkal	Gatekeeper of the house of **Ellil**
Kish	Ancient Mesopotamian city-state
Kishar	Mesopotamian goddess; mother of **Anu**; consort of **Anshar**
kor	A measure of liquid volume
Lahamu	A Mesopotamian goddess; mother of **Anshar** and **Kishar**
Lahmu	A Mesopotamian god; father of **Anshar** and **Kishar**
Lugalbanda	Father of **Gilgamesh**; treated as a deity in the *Epic of Gilgamesh*
Mami	A mother goddess; one of the **Annunaki**
Marduk	Chief Babylonian creator god and hero

mina	A measure of dry weight
Mount Nimush	Mountain where the ark of **Utnapishtim** comes to rest after the Great Flood
Mountain of Mashu	Mountain under which runs the path that **Shamash** takes during the night
Mummu	Adviser to the god **Apsu**
Namtar	Adviser to **Ereshkigal**; associated with plague and disease
Nanna	God of the moon; one of the **Annunaki**
Nergal	God of war and consort of **Ereshkigal**
Nibiru	The planet Jupiter
Ninsun	Mesopotamian goddess; mother of **Gilgamesh**
Nintu	A mother goddess who helps create the human race; one of the **Annunaki**
Ninurta	A hero-god; son of **Mami**
Nusku	Adviser to **Ellil**; associated with light and fire
Papsukkal	Counsellor and servant to the **Annunaki**
Qingu	Son of **Tiamat**; rises in rebellion against the gods and is killed by **Marduk**
Shamash	God of the sun; one of the **Annunaki**
Shamhat	Prostitute who civilizes **Enkidu**

Shara	A Sumerian god of war; son of Ishtar
Shuruppak	Ancient Sumerian city on the banks of the Euphrates
Siduri	An old woman who keeps a tavern near the seashore in the Epic of Gilgamesh
Sin	God of the moon; also known as **Nanna**; one of the **Annunaki**
Tammuz	A dying-and-rising god; consort of **Ishtar**
Tiamat	Mesopotamian goddess associated with salt water; rebels against the gods and is killed by **Marduk**, who uses her body to create the world
Urshanabi	Boatman to **Utnapishtim** in the *Epic of Gilgamesh*
Uruk	Ancient Sumerian city; **Gilgamesh** is its king in the *Epic of Gilgamesh*
Utnapishtim	Man who survives the Great Flood and is granted eternal life by the gods; character in the *Epic of Gilgamesh*
Waters of Death	Band of water in the ocean that separates the land of mortal people from the place where **Utnapishtim** lives in the *Epic of Gilgamesh*

Check out more mythology books by Matt Clayton

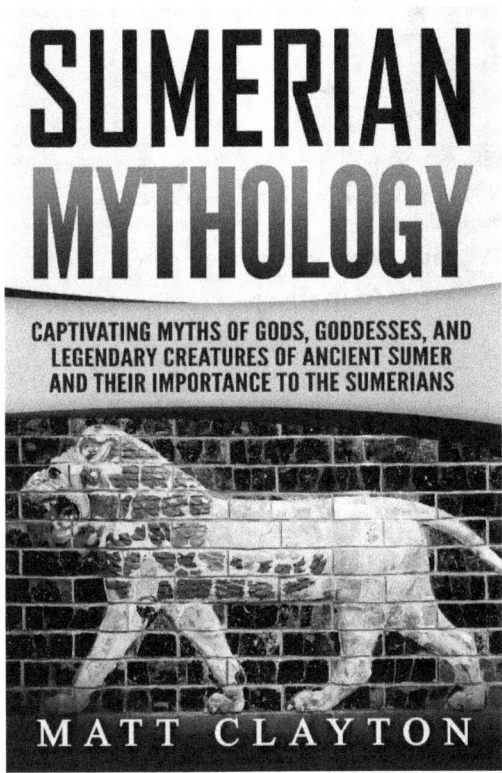

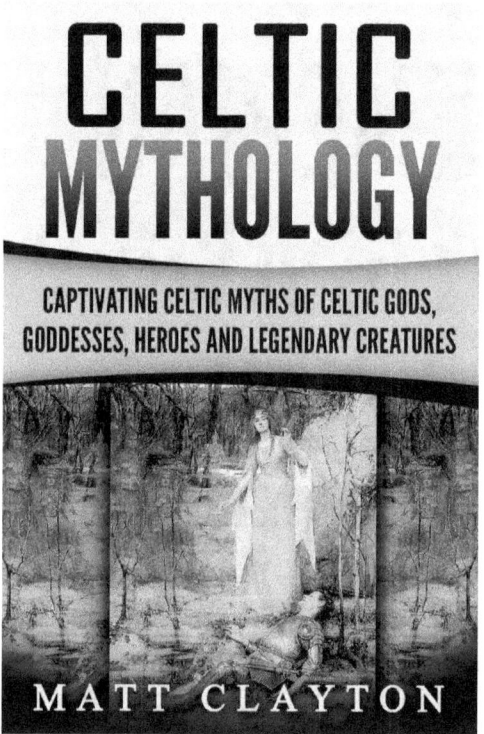

Bibliography

Dalley, Stephanie, trans. *Myths from Mesopotamia: Creation, The Flood, Gilgamesh, and Others*. Rev. ed. Oxford: Oxford University Press, 2000.

Ehrlich, Carl S., ed. *From an Antique Land: An Introduction to Ancient Near Eastern Literature*. Lanham: Rowman & Littlefield Publishers, Inc., 2009.

Ferry, David. *Gilgamesh: A New Rendering in English Verse*. New York: The Noonday Press, 1993.

Fessenden, Marissa. "Iraqi Museum Discovers Missing Lines from the Epic of Gilgamesh." **Smithsonian.com**, 7 October 2015.

Foster, Benjamin R. *Before the Muses: An Anthology of Akkadian Literature*. 3rd ed. Bethesda: CDL Press, 2005.

George, Andrew R. *The Babylonian Gilgamesh Epic*. Volume I: *Introduction, Critical Edition, and Cuneiform Texts*. Oxford: Oxford University Press, 2003.

Hallo, William W., ed. *The Context of Scripture: Canonical Compositions, Monumental Inscriptions, and Archival*

Documents from the Biblical World. 3 Vols. Boston: Brill, 2003.

Heidl, Alexander. *The Babylonian Genesis: The Story of Creation.* 2nd ed. Chicago: University of Chicago Press, 1963.

King, L. W. *The Seven Tablets of Creation: or, The Babylonian and Assyrian Legends Concerning the Creation of the World and of Mankind.* Vol. 1. London: Luzac and Co., 1902.

Lambert, W. G. *Babylonian Creation Myths.* Winona Lake: Eisenbrauns, 2013.

Langdon, Stephen Herbert. *Mythology of All Races.* Vol. 5: *Semitic.* New York: Cooper Square Publishers, 1964.

Leeming, David. *The Oxford Companion to World Mythology.* Oxford: Oxford University Press, 2005.

———. *The World of Myth: An Anthology.* Oxford: Oxford University Press, 1990.

Leick, Gwendolyn. *A Dictionary of Ancient Near Eastern Mythology.* London: Routledge, 1991.

Mason, Herbert. *Gilgamesh: A Verse Narrative.* New York: Mentor Books, 1972.

Mitchell, Stephen. *Gilgamesh: A New English Version.* New York: Free Press, 2004.

Pritchard, James B., ed. *Ancient Near Eastern Texts Relating to the Old Testament.* 3rd ed. Princeton: Princeton University Press, 1969.

Rogers, Robert William, trans. and ed. *Cuneiform Parallels to the Old Testament.* New York: Eaton & Mains, 1912.

Spence, Lewis. *Myths & Legends of Babylon and Assyria.* London: G. G. Harrap, 1916.